# 50 Plant-Based Dessert Recipes for Home

By: Kelly Johnson

## Table of Contents

- Vegan Chocolate Cake
- Coconut Milk Ice Cream
- Avocado Chocolate Mousse
- Chia Seed Pudding
- Vegan Banana Bread
- Almond Butter Cookies
- Pumpkin Pie Bars
- Mango Sorbet
- Vegan Cheesecake
- Lemon Poppy Seed Muffins
- Raspberry Oat Bars
- Carrot Cake Cupcakes
- Peanut Butter Chocolate Truffles
- Blueberry Crisp
- Vegan Tiramisu
- Almond Joy Energy Bites
- Matcha Green Tea Cookies
- Cashew Cream Tart
- Strawberry Shortcake
- Pineapple Coconut Nice Cream
- Chocolate Avocado Cookies
- Vanilla Bean Panna Cotta
- Apple Cinnamon Rolls
- Vegan Lemon Bars
- Hazelnut Chocolate Brownies
- Pecan Pie
- Key Lime Pie
- Caramelized Banana Ice Cream
- Vegan Rice Pudding
- Blackberry Cobbler
- Sweet Potato Pie
- Pistachio Rosewater Cookies
- Coconut Flour Pancakes
- Chocolate Chia Seed Pudding
- Vegan Oreo Cheesecake
- Lemon Lavender Cupcakes

- Almond Flour Blueberry Scones
- Chocolate Peanut Butter Fudge
- Mango Coconut Rice Pudding
- Raspberry Chocolate Chip Cookies
- Vegan Snickerdoodles
- Pumpkin Spice Donuts
- Orange Cardamom Cake
- Banana Nut Bread
- Berry Crumble Bars
- Gingerbread Cookies
- Kiwi Sorbet
- Vegan Bread Pudding
- Chocolate Covered Strawberries
- Maple Pecan Pie Bars

**Vegan Chocolate Cake**

**Ingredients:**

- 1 1/2 cups all-purpose flour
- 1 cup granulated sugar
- 1/4 cup cocoa powder
- 1 tsp baking soda
- 1/2 tsp salt
- 1 cup non-dairy milk (such as almond milk or soy milk)
- 1/3 cup vegetable oil
- 1 tbsp apple cider vinegar
- 1 tsp vanilla extract

**Instructions:**

1. Preheat your oven to 350°F (175°C). Grease and flour an 8-inch round cake pan.
2. In a large bowl, sift together the flour, sugar, cocoa powder, baking soda, and salt.
3. In a separate bowl, whisk together the non-dairy milk, vegetable oil, apple cider vinegar, and vanilla extract.
4. Pour the wet ingredients into the dry ingredients and stir until just combined. Be careful not to overmix.
5. Pour the batter into the prepared cake pan and spread it out evenly.
6. Bake in the preheated oven for 30-35 minutes, or until a toothpick inserted into the center comes out clean.
7. Remove from the oven and let the cake cool in the pan for about 10 minutes. Then, carefully transfer it to a wire rack to cool completely before frosting.

**Optional Frosting:**

For a simple vegan chocolate frosting, you can melt together:

- 1/2 cup vegan chocolate chips
- 1/4 cup non-dairy milk
- 1 tbsp maple syrup or powdered sugar

Melt the chocolate chips with the non-dairy milk over low heat, stirring constantly until smooth. Remove from heat and stir in maple syrup or powdered sugar until well combined. Let it cool slightly before spreading it over the cooled cake.

Enjoy your delicious Vegan Chocolate Cake!

**Coconut Milk Ice Cream**

**Ingredients:**

- 2 cans (14 oz each) full-fat coconut milk, chilled in the refrigerator overnight
- 1/2 cup maple syrup or agave syrup (adjust sweetness to taste)
- 1 tsp vanilla extract
- Pinch of salt
- Optional add-ins: chopped nuts, chocolate chips, fruit, etc.

**Instructions:**

1. **Chill Coconut Milk:** Place the cans of coconut milk in the refrigerator overnight. This helps separate the coconut cream from the liquid.
2. **Prepare the Base:** Open the chilled cans of coconut milk without shaking them. Scoop out the solid coconut cream that has risen to the top into a mixing bowl. Save the remaining coconut water for another use (smoothies, etc.).
3. **Mix Ingredients:** Add maple syrup (or agave syrup), vanilla extract, and a pinch of salt to the coconut cream. Use a hand mixer or whisk to blend until smooth and creamy. Taste and adjust sweetness if necessary.
4. **Churn:** If you have an ice cream maker, pour the mixture into the machine and churn according to the manufacturer's instructions until it reaches a soft-serve consistency. If you don't have an ice cream maker, proceed to the next step.
5. **Freeze:** Transfer the mixture into a freezer-safe container. Stir in any optional add-ins at this point. Cover the container with a lid or plastic wrap directly on the surface of the ice cream to prevent ice crystals from forming.
6. **Set:** Freeze the ice cream for at least 4-6 hours, or until firm.
7. **Serve:** Remove the ice cream from the freezer a few minutes before serving to soften slightly. Scoop and enjoy your creamy Coconut Milk Ice Cream!

This recipe yields a rich and creamy vegan dessert with the delightful flavor of coconut. Feel free to customize it with your favorite toppings or mix-ins for added texture and taste.

**Avocado Chocolate Mousse**

**Ingredients:**

- 2 ripe avocados
- 1/4 cup cocoa powder (unsweetened)
- 1/4 cup maple syrup or agave syrup (adjust to taste)
- 1 tsp vanilla extract
- Pinch of salt
- Optional toppings: fresh berries, chopped nuts, coconut flakes

**Instructions:**

1. **Prepare Avocados:** Cut the avocados in half, remove the pits, and scoop the flesh into a food processor or blender.
2. **Blend:** Add cocoa powder, maple syrup (or agave syrup), vanilla extract, and a pinch of salt to the avocados.
3. **Blend Until Smooth:** Blend all the ingredients until smooth and creamy. Stop to scrape down the sides of the processor or blender if needed to ensure everything is well incorporated.
4. **Taste and Adjust:** Taste the mousse and adjust sweetness as desired by adding more maple syrup or agave syrup.
5. **Chill:** Transfer the avocado chocolate mousse into serving bowls or glasses. Cover and refrigerate for at least 30 minutes to chill and firm up.
6. **Serve:** Before serving, you can garnish with fresh berries, chopped nuts, or coconut flakes for added texture and flavor.

Avocado Chocolate Mousse is rich, creamy, and naturally sweetened, making it a guilt-free treat that's packed with healthy fats from avocados. Enjoy this delicious dessert!

## Chia Seed Pudding

### Ingredients:

- 1/4 cup chia seeds
- 1 cup non-dairy milk (such as almond milk, coconut milk, soy milk)
- 1-2 tbsp maple syrup or agave syrup (adjust to taste)
- 1/2 tsp vanilla extract
- Optional toppings: fresh fruit, nuts, seeds, coconut flakes, etc.

### Instructions:

1. **Mix Ingredients:** In a bowl or jar, combine chia seeds, non-dairy milk, maple syrup (or agave syrup), and vanilla extract. Stir well to combine.
2. **Let it Sit:** Cover the bowl or jar and refrigerate for at least 2 hours, or preferably overnight. This allows the chia seeds to absorb the liquid and create a pudding-like consistency.
3. **Stir Again:** After the initial refrigeration period, give the mixture a good stir to break up any clumps and distribute the chia seeds evenly.
4. **Serve:** Spoon the chia seed pudding into serving bowls or glasses. Top with your favorite toppings such as fresh fruit, nuts, seeds, or coconut flakes.
5. **Enjoy:** Chia seed pudding can be enjoyed chilled straight from the refrigerator. It's a versatile dish that can be eaten for breakfast, as a snack, or as a dessert.

### Variations:

- **Chocolate Chia Seed Pudding:** Add 1-2 tbsp of cocoa powder or melted chocolate to the mixture before refrigerating.
- **Fruit Flavored:** Blend in fresh or frozen fruit such as berries or mango before refrigerating for a fruity twist.
- **Matcha Chia Seed Pudding:** Mix in 1-2 tsp of matcha powder for a vibrant green tea flavor.

Chia seed pudding is not only delicious but also packed with fiber, healthy fats, and plant-based protein, making it a nutritious addition to your diet.

**Vegan Banana Bread**

**Ingredients:**

- 4 ripe bananas, mashed
- 1/3 cup melted coconut oil or vegetable oil
- 1/2 cup maple syrup or agave syrup
- 1/4 cup non-dairy milk (such as almond milk or soy milk)
- 1 tsp vanilla extract
- 2 cups all-purpose flour
- 1 tsp baking soda
- 1/2 tsp salt
- 1/2 tsp ground cinnamon (optional)
- Optional add-ins: chopped nuts, chocolate chips, dried fruit

**Instructions:**

1. **Preheat** your oven to 350°F (175°C). Grease a 9x5 inch loaf pan or line it with parchment paper.
2. **Mix Wet Ingredients:** In a large bowl, mash the ripe bananas with a fork until smooth. Add melted coconut oil (or vegetable oil), maple syrup (or agave syrup), non-dairy milk, and vanilla extract. Mix well until combined.
3. **Combine Dry Ingredients:** In a separate bowl, whisk together the flour, baking soda, salt, and cinnamon (if using).
4. **Combine Mixtures:** Gradually add the dry ingredients to the wet ingredients, stirring until just combined. Be careful not to overmix. If using any add-ins like nuts or chocolate chips, fold them into the batter gently.
5. **Bake:** Pour the batter into the prepared loaf pan and spread it out evenly. Bake in the preheated oven for 55-65 minutes, or until a toothpick inserted into the center comes out clean.
6. **Cool:** Remove the banana bread from the oven and let it cool in the pan for about 10 minutes. Then, transfer it to a wire rack to cool completely before slicing.
7. **Serve:** Slice and enjoy your delicious vegan banana bread!

This recipe results in a moist and flavorful banana bread that's perfect for breakfast, as a snack, or even dessert. It's vegan-friendly and can be customized with your favorite mix-ins for added texture and taste.

## Almond Butter Cookies

### Ingredients:

- 1 cup almond butter (creamy or crunchy, unsweetened)
- 1/2 cup coconut sugar or brown sugar
- 1 flax egg (1 tbsp ground flaxseed meal + 3 tbsp water)
- 1 tsp vanilla extract
- 1/2 tsp baking soda
- 1/4 tsp salt
- Optional: 1/2 cup dairy-free chocolate chips, chopped nuts, or dried fruit

### Instructions:

1. **Preheat** your oven to 350°F (175°C). Line a baking sheet with parchment paper.
2. **Make Flax Egg:** In a small bowl, combine ground flaxseed meal and water. Stir well and let it sit for about 5 minutes to thicken.
3. **Mix Wet Ingredients:** In a mixing bowl, combine almond butter, coconut sugar (or brown sugar), flax egg, and vanilla extract. Mix until well combined.
4. **Add Dry Ingredients:** Add baking soda and salt to the almond butter mixture. Stir until thoroughly combined. If you're adding optional ingredients like chocolate chips or nuts, fold them into the dough at this point.
5. **Form Cookies:** Scoop about 1 tablespoon of dough for each cookie and roll into balls. Place them on the prepared baking sheet, leaving some space between each cookie.
6. **Flatten Cookies:** Using a fork, gently press down on each cookie to create a crisscross pattern.
7. **Bake:** Bake in the preheated oven for 10-12 minutes, or until the edges are lightly golden.
8. **Cool:** Remove from the oven and let the cookies cool on the baking sheet for 5 minutes. Then, transfer them to a wire rack to cool completely.
9. **Enjoy:** Once cooled, enjoy your vegan almond butter cookies! Store any leftovers in an airtight container at room temperature for up to a week.

These almond butter cookies are soft and chewy with a delightful nutty flavor. They're perfect for sharing or enjoying as a snack any time of day.

## Pumpkin Pie Bars

**Ingredients:**

**For the Crust:**

- 1 1/2 cups graham cracker crumbs (use vegan graham crackers if needed)
- 1/4 cup coconut oil, melted (or vegan butter)
- 2 tbsp maple syrup or agave syrup
- Pinch of salt

**For the Pumpkin Filling:**

- 1 can (15 oz) pumpkin puree (not pumpkin pie filling)
- 1/2 cup full-fat coconut milk (from a can)
- 1/2 cup maple syrup or agave syrup
- 1/4 cup cornstarch or arrowroot powder
- 1 tsp vanilla extract
- 1 1/2 tsp ground cinnamon
- 1/2 tsp ground ginger
- 1/4 tsp ground nutmeg
- 1/4 tsp ground cloves
- Pinch of salt

**Instructions:**

1. **Preheat** your oven to 350°F (175°C). Line an 8x8 inch baking dish with parchment paper, leaving some overhang for easy removal later.
2. **Make the Crust:**
   - In a bowl, combine graham cracker crumbs, melted coconut oil (or vegan butter), maple syrup (or agave syrup), and a pinch of salt. Mix until the crumbs are evenly coated and resemble wet sand.
   - Press the mixture firmly and evenly into the bottom of the prepared baking dish.
3. **Bake the Crust:**
   - Bake the crust in the preheated oven for 10 minutes. Remove from the oven and set aside while you prepare the filling.
4. **Make the Pumpkin Filling:**
   - In a large bowl, whisk together the pumpkin puree, coconut milk, maple syrup (or agave syrup), cornstarch (or arrowroot powder), vanilla extract, spices (cinnamon, ginger, nutmeg, cloves), and a pinch of salt until smooth and well combined.
5. **Assemble and Bake:**
   - Pour the pumpkin filling over the pre-baked crust, spreading it out evenly with a spatula.

- Return the baking dish to the oven and bake for 45-50 minutes, or until the edges are set and the center is slightly jiggly.
- Remove from the oven and let the pumpkin pie bars cool completely in the baking dish on a wire rack. Once cooled, refrigerate for at least 2 hours (or overnight) to firm up.

6. **Serve:**
   - Lift the chilled pumpkin pie bars out of the baking dish using the parchment paper overhang. Slice into bars and serve chilled.
   - Optionally, dust with powdered sugar or serve with a dollop of whipped coconut cream.

These vegan pumpkin pie bars are creamy, spiced perfectly, and make a delightful dessert for any fall gathering or Thanksgiving feast. Enjoy the flavors of autumn in every bite!

**Mango Sorbet**

**Ingredients:**

- 4 cups frozen mango chunks
- 1/2 cup coconut milk (full-fat, from a can)
- 1/4 cup maple syrup or agave syrup (adjust to taste)
- 1 tbsp lime juice (optional, for a tangy twist)

**Instructions:**

1. **Prepare Mango:** If you haven't already, freeze the mango chunks until solid. Frozen mango works best for achieving a smooth sorbet texture.
2. **Blend Ingredients:** In a blender or food processor, combine the frozen mango chunks, coconut milk, maple syrup (or agave syrup), and lime juice (if using). Blend until smooth and creamy. You may need to stop and scrape down the sides of the blender a few times to ensure everything is well combined.
3. **Taste and Adjust:** Taste the mixture and adjust sweetness or tartness to your preference by adding more maple syrup/agave syrup or lime juice.
4. **Chill:** Transfer the blended mixture to a freezer-safe container. Cover and freeze for at least 4 hours, or until firm.
5. **Serve:** Remove the mango sorbet from the freezer a few minutes before serving to soften slightly. Scoop into bowls or cones and enjoy!

**Optional Additions:**

- **Fresh Mango:** Add a few pieces of fresh diced mango into the blender along with the frozen mango for added texture.
- **Coconut Flakes:** Sprinkle toasted coconut flakes on top before serving for extra flavor and crunch.

This vegan mango sorbet is dairy-free, naturally gluten-free, and bursting with tropical mango flavor. It's a delightful treat that's both easy to make and incredibly satisfying on a warm day.

# Vegan Cheesecake

## Ingredients:

### For the Crust:

- 1 1/2 cups graham cracker crumbs (use vegan graham crackers if needed)
- 1/4 cup melted coconut oil or vegan butter
- 2 tbsp maple syrup or agave syrup

### For the Filling:

- 2 cups raw cashews (soaked in water for at least 4 hours or overnight, then drained)
- 1/2 cup full-fat coconut milk (from a can)
- 1/2 cup maple syrup or agave syrup
- 1/3 cup melted coconut oil
- 1/4 cup fresh lemon juice
- 1 tsp vanilla extract
- Pinch of salt

### For Topping (optional):

- Fresh berries, fruit compote, or vegan whipped cream

## Instructions:

1. **Prepare the Crust:**
   - Preheat your oven to 350°F (175°C). Grease a 9-inch springform pan or line it with parchment paper.
   - In a bowl, mix together graham cracker crumbs, melted coconut oil (or vegan butter), and maple syrup (or agave syrup) until well combined and the mixture resembles wet sand.
   - Press the mixture evenly into the bottom of the prepared pan.
2. **Bake the Crust:**
   - Bake the crust in the preheated oven for 10 minutes. Remove from the oven and set aside to cool while you prepare the filling.
3. **Make the Filling:**
   - In a high-speed blender or food processor, combine soaked and drained cashews, coconut milk, maple syrup (or agave syrup), melted coconut oil, lemon juice, vanilla extract, and a pinch of salt.
   - Blend on high until the mixture is smooth and creamy, scraping down the sides as needed to ensure everything is well blended.
4. **Assemble the Cheesecake:**
   - Pour the filling over the cooled crust in the springform pan. Use a spatula to smooth out the top.
5. **Chill:**

- Cover the cheesecake with plastic wrap or a lid and place it in the refrigerator to set for at least 4-6 hours, or preferably overnight.
6. **Serve:**
    - Once chilled and set, carefully remove the sides of the springform pan. Slice the vegan cheesecake into pieces and serve chilled.
    - Optionally, top each slice with fresh berries, fruit compote, or a dollop of vegan whipped cream before serving.

This vegan cheesecake is rich, creamy, and has a smooth texture similar to traditional cheesecake but without any dairy or animal products. It's perfect for special occasions or as a delightful dessert any time!

## Lemon Poppy Seed Muffins

**Ingredients:**

- 2 cups all-purpose flour
- 1/2 cup granulated sugar
- 2 tbsp poppy seeds
- 1 tbsp baking powder
- 1/2 tsp baking soda
- 1/4 tsp salt
- 1 cup non-dairy milk (such as almond milk or soy milk)
- 1/2 cup lemon juice (freshly squeezed)
- 1/3 cup melted coconut oil or vegetable oil
- Zest of 2 lemons
- 1 tsp vanilla extract

**For the Glaze (optional):**

- 1/2 cup powdered sugar
- 1-2 tbsp lemon juice

**Instructions:**

1. **Preheat** your oven to 375°F (190°C). Line a muffin tin with paper liners or grease the cups lightly.
2. **Prepare Dry Ingredients:** In a large bowl, whisk together the flour, sugar, poppy seeds, baking powder, baking soda, and salt.
3. **Combine Wet Ingredients:** In a separate bowl, mix together the non-dairy milk, lemon juice, melted coconut oil (or vegetable oil), lemon zest, and vanilla extract.
4. **Combine Mixtures:** Pour the wet ingredients into the dry ingredients. Stir until just combined, being careful not to overmix. The batter will be thick and slightly lumpy.
5. **Fill Muffin Cups:** Divide the batter evenly among the muffin cups, filling each about 2/3 full.
6. **Bake:** Bake in the preheated oven for 18-20 minutes, or until a toothpick inserted into the center comes out clean.
7. **Cool:** Remove the muffin tin from the oven and let the muffins cool in the tin for 5 minutes. Then, transfer them to a wire rack to cool completely.
8. **Prepare Glaze (optional):**
   - In a small bowl, whisk together powdered sugar and lemon juice until smooth and drizzle-able.
9. **Glaze Muffins (optional):**
   - Once the muffins are completely cooled, drizzle the glaze over the tops using a spoon or fork.
10. **Serve:** Enjoy your vegan lemon poppy seed muffins!

These muffins are bursting with lemon flavor from both the juice and zest, and the poppy seeds add a nice crunch. They are perfect for a light breakfast or a delightful snack any time of day.

**Raspberry Oat Bars**

**Ingredients:**

**For the Raspberry Filling:**

- 2 cups fresh or frozen raspberries
- 2 tbsp maple syrup or agave syrup
- 1 tbsp lemon juice
- 1 tbsp cornstarch or arrowroot powder

**For the Oat Base and Crumble:**

- 1 1/2 cups rolled oats (use gluten-free oats if needed)
- 1 cup all-purpose flour (or whole wheat flour)
- 1/2 cup coconut sugar or brown sugar
- 1/2 tsp baking powder
- 1/4 tsp salt
- 1/2 cup melted coconut oil or vegan butter
- 1 tsp vanilla extract

**Instructions:**

1. **Preheat** your oven to 350°F (175°C). Grease or line an 8x8 inch baking dish with parchment paper.
2. **Make the Raspberry Filling:**
   - In a saucepan, combine raspberries, maple syrup (or agave syrup), and lemon juice over medium heat.
   - Cook for about 5 minutes, stirring occasionally, until the raspberries break down and release their juices.
   - In a small bowl, mix cornstarch (or arrowroot powder) with a tablespoon of water to create a slurry. Stir the slurry into the raspberry mixture and cook for another 1-2 minutes until thickened.
   - Remove from heat and set aside to cool slightly.
3. **Prepare the Oat Base and Crumble:**
   - In a large bowl, combine rolled oats, flour, coconut sugar (or brown sugar), baking powder, and salt.
   - Add melted coconut oil (or vegan butter) and vanilla extract to the dry ingredients. Mix until the mixture is crumbly and well combined.
4. **Assemble the Bars:**
   - Press about two-thirds of the oat mixture evenly into the bottom of the prepared baking dish to form the base.
   - Spread the raspberry filling evenly over the oat base.
5. **Add the Crumble Topping:**

- Sprinkle the remaining oat mixture evenly over the raspberry filling, covering it as much as possible.
6. **Bake:**
    - Bake in the preheated oven for 30-35 minutes, or until the top is golden brown and the raspberry filling is bubbling.
7. **Cool and Serve:**
    - Remove from the oven and let the raspberry oat bars cool completely in the baking dish on a wire rack.
    - Once cooled, lift the bars out of the dish using the parchment paper overhang. Cut into squares and serve.

These vegan raspberry oat bars are chewy, sweet, and tart, making them a delightful treat for breakfast or as a snack. Store any leftovers in an airtight container at room temperature or in the refrigerator. Enjoy!

# Carrot Cake Cupcakes

**Ingredients:**

**For the Cupcakes:**

- 1 1/2 cups grated carrots (about 2-3 medium carrots)
- 1 cup all-purpose flour
- 1/2 cup whole wheat flour (or additional all-purpose flour)
- 1 cup coconut sugar or brown sugar
- 1/2 cup chopped walnuts or pecans (optional)
- 1/2 cup raisins (optional)
- 1 tsp baking powder
- 1/2 tsp baking soda
- 1/2 tsp salt
- 1 tsp ground cinnamon
- 1/2 tsp ground nutmeg
- 1/2 cup unsweetened applesauce
- 1/2 cup non-dairy milk (such as almond milk or soy milk)
- 1/3 cup melted coconut oil or vegetable oil
- 1 tsp vanilla extract

**For the Frosting:**

- 1/2 cup vegan butter, softened
- 1 1/2 cups powdered sugar
- 1 tsp vanilla extract
- 1-2 tbsp non-dairy milk (if needed to adjust consistency)

**Instructions:**

1. **Preheat** your oven to 350°F (175°C). Line a muffin tin with paper liners or grease the cups lightly.
2. **Prepare Carrots:** Grate the carrots using a box grater or food processor. Set aside.
3. **Make the Cupcake Batter:**
    - In a large bowl, whisk together the all-purpose flour, whole wheat flour (if using), coconut sugar (or brown sugar), chopped nuts (if using), raisins (if using), baking powder, baking soda, salt, ground cinnamon, and ground nutmeg.
    - In a separate bowl, whisk together the applesauce, non-dairy milk, melted coconut oil (or vegetable oil), and vanilla extract.
    - Pour the wet ingredients into the dry ingredients and stir until just combined. Fold in the grated carrots until evenly distributed.
4. **Fill Muffin Cups:** Spoon the batter evenly into the prepared muffin cups, filling each about 3/4 full.

5. **Bake:** Bake in the preheated oven for 20-25 minutes, or until a toothpick inserted into the center of a cupcake comes out clean.
6. **Cool:** Remove the muffin tin from the oven and let the cupcakes cool in the tin for 5 minutes. Then, transfer them to a wire rack to cool completely.
7. **Make the Frosting:**
    - In a mixing bowl, beat the softened vegan butter until smooth and creamy.
    - Gradually add powdered sugar, a little at a time, and continue to beat until well combined.
    - Add vanilla extract and non-dairy milk (if needed) to achieve a smooth and spreadable consistency.
8. **Frost the Cupcakes:**
    - Once the cupcakes are completely cooled, frost them with the vegan buttercream frosting using a spatula or piping bag.
9. **Serve:** Optionally, garnish with chopped nuts or a sprinkle of cinnamon on top of the frosting.

These vegan carrot cake cupcakes are moist, flavorful, and topped with a creamy frosting that complements the spices and sweetness of the cake. They make a perfect treat for any occasion!

## Peanut Butter Chocolate Truffles

### Ingredients:

- 1/2 cup creamy peanut butter (unsweetened)
- 2 tbsp maple syrup or agave syrup (adjust to taste)
- 2 tbsp coconut flour (or almond flour)
- 1/2 cup dairy-free chocolate chips
- 1 tbsp coconut oil
- Optional toppings: crushed peanuts, shredded coconut, cocoa powder

### Instructions:

1. **Prepare the Peanut Butter Filling:**
   - In a mixing bowl, combine the creamy peanut butter, maple syrup (or agave syrup), and coconut flour (or almond flour). Mix until well combined and a dough-like consistency forms.
   - If the mixture is too sticky, add more coconut flour a teaspoon at a time until you can easily roll the dough into balls.
2. **Roll into Balls:**
   - Roll the peanut butter mixture into small balls, about 1 inch in diameter. Place them on a parchment-lined baking sheet. Place the baking sheet in the freezer for about 15-20 minutes to firm up the balls.
3. **Prepare the Chocolate Coating:**
   - In a microwave-safe bowl or using a double boiler, melt the dairy-free chocolate chips and coconut oil together until smooth and well combined. Stir occasionally to prevent burning.
4. **Coat the Truffles:**
   - Remove the peanut butter balls from the freezer. Using a fork or dipping tool, dip each ball into the melted chocolate mixture, making sure to coat it completely.
   - Tap off any excess chocolate and place the coated truffle back onto the parchment-lined baking sheet.
5. **Optional Toppings:**
   - While the chocolate coating is still wet, sprinkle the truffles with crushed peanuts, shredded coconut, or dust with cocoa powder for decoration.
6. **Chill and Serve:**
   - Place the baking sheet with the coated truffles in the refrigerator for about 30 minutes, or until the chocolate coating is set.
   - Once set, transfer the truffles to an airtight container and store in the refrigerator until ready to serve.

These Vegan Peanut Butter Chocolate Truffles are rich, creamy, and decadent, with the perfect balance of peanut butter and chocolate flavors. They make a wonderful homemade gift or a delightful treat for any occasion!

**Blueberry Crisp**

**Ingredients:**

**For the Blueberry Filling:**

- 4 cups fresh or frozen blueberries
- 1/4 cup maple syrup or agave syrup (adjust to taste depending on sweetness of berries)
- 1 tbsp lemon juice
- 1 tbsp cornstarch or arrowroot powder
- Zest of 1 lemon (optional)

**For the Oat Topping:**

- 1 cup rolled oats (use gluten-free oats if needed)
- 1/2 cup almond flour or all-purpose flour
- 1/2 cup chopped nuts (such as almonds, pecans, or walnuts)
- 1/4 cup coconut sugar or brown sugar
- 1/4 cup melted coconut oil or vegan butter
- 1 tsp ground cinnamon
- Pinch of salt

**Instructions:**

1. **Preheat** your oven to 350°F (175°C). Grease an 8x8 inch baking dish or a similar-sized baking dish with coconut oil or vegan butter.
2. **Prepare the Blueberry Filling:**
   - In a large bowl, combine the blueberries, maple syrup (or agave syrup), lemon juice, cornstarch (or arrowroot powder), and lemon zest (if using). Stir gently until the blueberries are evenly coated.
3. **Transfer to Baking Dish:**
   - Pour the blueberry mixture into the prepared baking dish and spread it out evenly.
4. **Make the Oat Topping:**
   - In a separate bowl, combine rolled oats, almond flour (or all-purpose flour), chopped nuts, coconut sugar (or brown sugar), melted coconut oil (or vegan butter), ground cinnamon, and a pinch of salt. Mix until the mixture is crumbly and well combined.
5. **Top the Blueberries:**
   - Sprinkle the oat topping evenly over the blueberry filling in the baking dish, covering it completely.
6. **Bake:**
   - Bake in the preheated oven for 35-40 minutes, or until the blueberry filling is bubbly and the oat topping is golden brown.
7. **Cool and Serve:**

- Remove from the oven and let the blueberry crisp cool slightly before serving.
- Serve warm, optionally with a scoop of dairy-free vanilla ice cream or coconut whipped cream.

This Vegan Blueberry Crisp is a delightful dessert that showcases the natural sweetness of blueberries with a crunchy, oat-studded topping. It's perfect for any occasion and can be enjoyed as a comforting treat year-round!

# Vegan Tiramisu

## Ingredients:

### For the Cashew Mascarpone:

- 1 1/2 cups raw cashews (soaked in water for at least 4 hours or overnight, then drained)
- 1/4 cup coconut cream (from a can)
- 1/4 cup maple syrup or agave syrup
- 2 tbsp lemon juice
- 1 tsp vanilla extract
- Pinch of salt

### For the Coffee Soaking Liquid:

- 1 cup brewed strong coffee, cooled to room temperature
- 2 tbsp coffee liqueur (optional)
- 1-2 tbsp maple syrup or agave syrup (optional, adjust to taste)

### For Assembling:

- 1 package vegan ladyfinger cookies (approx. 24 cookies)
- Cocoa powder, for dusting

## Instructions:

1. **Prepare the Cashew Mascarpone:**
    - In a high-speed blender or food processor, combine soaked and drained cashews, coconut cream, maple syrup (or agave syrup), lemon juice, vanilla extract, and a pinch of salt.
    - Blend until smooth and creamy, scraping down the sides as needed to ensure everything is well combined. The consistency should be similar to traditional mascarpone cheese.
2. **Prepare the Coffee Soaking Liquid:**
    - In a shallow bowl, mix together brewed strong coffee and coffee liqueur (if using). Optionally, sweeten with maple syrup or agave syrup to taste.
3. **Assemble the Tiramisu:**
    - Dip each vegan ladyfinger cookie into the coffee soaking liquid briefly, making sure not to soak them too much as they can become too soggy.
    - Arrange a layer of soaked ladyfinger cookies in the bottom of a square or rectangular dish (about 8x8 inches).
4. **Layer with Cashew Mascarpone:**
    - Spread half of the cashew mascarpone mixture evenly over the soaked ladyfingers, using a spatula to smooth it out.
5. **Repeat Layers:**

- Arrange another layer of soaked ladyfinger cookies over the cashew mascarpone.
- Spread the remaining cashew mascarpone mixture evenly over the cookies.

6. **Chill and Set:**
   - Cover the tiramisu with plastic wrap and refrigerate for at least 4 hours, or preferably overnight, to allow the flavors to meld and the dessert to set.

7. **Serve:**
   - Before serving, dust the top of the tiramisu generously with cocoa powder using a fine-mesh sieve.

8. **Enjoy:**
   - Slice and serve the vegan tiramisu chilled. It's a delightful dessert with layers of creamy cashew mascarpone and coffee-soaked ladyfingers, perfect for any occasion!

This vegan tiramisu recipe captures the essence of the traditional dessert while using plant-based ingredients for a creamy and indulgent treat.

# Almond Joy Energy Bites

**Ingredients:**

- 1 cup rolled oats
- 1/2 cup almond butter (creamy)
- 1/4 cup maple syrup or agave syrup
- 1/4 cup shredded coconut (unsweetened)
- 1/4 cup dairy-free chocolate chips
- 1/4 cup chopped almonds
- 1 tsp vanilla extract
- Pinch of salt

**Instructions:**

1. **Mix Ingredients:**
   - In a large mixing bowl, combine rolled oats, almond butter, maple syrup (or agave syrup), shredded coconut, dairy-free chocolate chips, chopped almonds, vanilla extract, and a pinch of salt.
2. **Combine Well:**
   - Mix all ingredients together until well combined. The mixture should be sticky and hold together when pressed.
3. **Form Balls:**
   - Using your hands, scoop about 1 tablespoon of the mixture and roll it into a ball between your palms. If the mixture is too sticky to handle, you can wet your hands slightly with water.
4. **Chill:**
   - Place the energy bites on a plate or baking sheet lined with parchment paper. Repeat until all the mixture is used.
   - Place the plate or baking sheet in the refrigerator for about 30 minutes to allow the energy bites to firm up.
5. **Store:**
   - Once chilled and firm, transfer the almond joy energy bites to an airtight container.
   - Store in the refrigerator for up to 2 weeks. You can also store them in the freezer for longer storage.

These Vegan Almond Joy Energy Bites are perfect for a quick snack or a healthy treat on the go. They're packed with oats, almond butter, coconut, and chocolate, providing a satisfying and nutritious bite-sized snack!

**Matcha Green Tea Cookies**

**Ingredients:**

- 1 1/2 cups all-purpose flour
- 2 tbsp matcha green tea powder
- 1/2 tsp baking powder
- 1/4 tsp salt
- 1/2 cup coconut oil, softened (or vegan butter)
- 3/4 cup powdered sugar
- 1 tsp vanilla extract
- 2-3 tbsp non-dairy milk (such as almond milk or soy milk)

**Instructions:**

1. **Preheat** your oven to 350°F (175°C). Line a baking sheet with parchment paper.
2. **Prepare Dry Ingredients:**
    - In a bowl, whisk together the all-purpose flour, matcha green tea powder, baking powder, and salt. Set aside.
3. **Cream Wet Ingredients:**
    - In a separate bowl, using a hand mixer or stand mixer, cream together the softened coconut oil (or vegan butter) and powdered sugar until light and fluffy.
    - Add vanilla extract and mix until combined.
4. **Combine and Form Dough:**
    - Gradually add the dry ingredients to the wet ingredients, mixing on low speed until well combined. The dough should come together and be slightly sticky.
    - If the dough is too dry, add 1 tablespoon of non-dairy milk at a time until you reach a smooth dough consistency.
5. **Shape Cookies:**
    - Scoop about 1 tablespoon of dough and roll it into a ball. Place it on the prepared baking sheet. Repeat with the remaining dough, spacing the cookies about 2 inches apart.
6. **Flatten Cookies (Optional):**
    - Using the bottom of a glass or your palm, gently flatten each cookie to about 1/4 inch thick.
7. **Bake:**
    - Bake in the preheated oven for 10-12 minutes, or until the edges are set and slightly golden.
    - Remove from the oven and let the cookies cool on the baking sheet for 5 minutes, then transfer them to a wire rack to cool completely.
8. **Serve:**
    - Once cooled, serve and enjoy your Vegan Matcha Green Tea Cookies!

These cookies have a subtle, earthy flavor from the matcha green tea powder and a wonderful soft texture. They are perfect for tea time or as a light dessert. Store any leftovers in an airtight container at room temperature for up to a week.

# Cashew Cream Tart

**Ingredients:**

**For the Nut Crust:**

- 1 1/2 cups raw nuts (such as almonds, walnuts, or a mix)
- 1/4 cup coconut oil, melted
- 2 tbsp maple syrup or agave syrup
- Pinch of salt

**For the Cashew Cream Filling:**

- 1 1/2 cups raw cashews (soaked in water for at least 4 hours or overnight, then drained)
- 1/2 cup full-fat coconut milk (from a can)
- 1/4 cup maple syrup or agave syrup (adjust to taste)
- 1/4 cup melted coconut oil
- 1 tsp vanilla extract
- Zest and juice of 1 lemon (optional, for tanginess)

**For Topping (Optional):**

- Fresh berries, sliced fruits, or a sprinkle of cocoa powder

**Instructions:**

1. **Prepare the Nut Crust:**
   - Preheat your oven to 350°F (175°C).
   - In a food processor, pulse the raw nuts until finely ground.
   - Add melted coconut oil, maple syrup (or agave syrup), and a pinch of salt. Pulse again until the mixture resembles coarse crumbs and sticks together when pressed.
2. **Form the Crust:**
   - Press the nut mixture firmly and evenly into the bottom and up the sides of a tart pan (about 9 inches in diameter). Use the back of a spoon or your fingers to pack it tightly.
3. **Bake the Crust:**
   - Bake the crust in the preheated oven for 10-12 minutes, or until lightly golden and fragrant. Remove from the oven and let it cool completely on a wire rack.
4. **Prepare the Cashew Cream Filling:**
   - In a high-speed blender, combine soaked and drained cashews, full-fat coconut milk, maple syrup (or agave syrup), melted coconut oil, vanilla extract, and lemon zest/juice (if using).
   - Blend on high until the mixture is smooth and creamy, scraping down the sides as needed to ensure everything is well combined.
5. **Assemble the Tart:**

- Pour the cashew cream filling into the cooled nut crust, spreading it out evenly with a spatula.
6. **Chill:**
    - Cover the tart with plastic wrap or foil and refrigerate for at least 4 hours, or until the filling is firm.
7. **Serve:**
    - Before serving, optionally decorate the tart with fresh berries, sliced fruits, or a sprinkle of cocoa powder.
8. **Enjoy:**
    - Slice and serve the cashew cream tart chilled. It's a creamy, indulgent dessert that's both satisfying and dairy-free!

This Cashew Cream Tart is perfect for special occasions or as a refreshing dessert on a warm day. The cashew cream filling provides a smooth texture with a hint of nuttiness, complementing the nutty crust beautifully.

**Strawberry Shortcake**

**Ingredients:**

**For the Biscuits:**

- 2 cups all-purpose flour
- 1 tbsp baking powder
- 1/4 tsp baking soda
- 1/2 tsp salt
- 1/4 cup granulated sugar
- 1/2 cup vegan butter (cold, cut into small pieces)
- 3/4 cup non-dairy milk (such as almond milk or soy milk)
- 1 tsp vanilla extract
- Zest of 1 lemon (optional)

**For the Strawberry Filling:**

- 4 cups fresh strawberries, hulled and sliced
- 2-3 tbsp maple syrup or agave syrup (adjust to taste)
- 1 tsp vanilla extract

**For the Coconut Whipped Cream:**

- 1 can (14 oz) full-fat coconut milk, chilled in the refrigerator overnight
- 1-2 tbsp powdered sugar (optional, for sweetness)
- 1 tsp vanilla extract

**Instructions:**

1. **Make the Biscuits:**
    - Preheat your oven to 425°F (220°C). Line a baking sheet with parchment paper.
    - In a large bowl, whisk together the flour, baking powder, baking soda, salt, and granulated sugar.
    - Add the cold vegan butter pieces to the flour mixture. Using a pastry cutter or fork, cut the butter into the flour until the mixture resembles coarse crumbs.
    - In a separate bowl, whisk together the non-dairy milk, vanilla extract, and lemon zest (if using).
    - Pour the wet ingredients into the dry ingredients and stir until just combined. Be careful not to overmix.
    - Turn the dough out onto a lightly floured surface and gently knead it a few times until it comes together.
    - Pat the dough into a circle about 1 inch thick. Use a round cookie cutter or a glass to cut out biscuits. Place them on the prepared baking sheet, spacing them about 1 inch apart.
    - Gather any remaining dough, gently pat it together, and cut out more biscuits.

2. **Bake the Biscuits:**
   - Bake in the preheated oven for 12-15 minutes, or until the biscuits are golden brown on top. Remove from the oven and let them cool on a wire rack.
3. **Prepare the Strawberry Filling:**
   - In a bowl, toss together the sliced strawberries, maple syrup (or agave syrup), and vanilla extract. Set aside to macerate while you prepare the whipped cream.
4. **Make the Coconut Whipped Cream:**
   - Open the chilled can of coconut milk and scoop out the solid coconut cream that has risen to the top (save the coconut water for another use, like smoothies).
   - Place the solid coconut cream in a chilled mixing bowl. Add powdered sugar (if using) and vanilla extract.
   - Whip the coconut cream with a hand mixer or stand mixer until fluffy and peaks form. Be careful not to overmix.
5. **Assemble the Strawberry Shortcake:**
   - Slice each biscuit in half horizontally. Place the bottom half on a plate.
   - Spoon some of the macerated strawberries over the biscuit bottom.
   - Dollop a generous amount of coconut whipped cream over the strawberries.
   - Place the top half of the biscuit on top of the whipped cream.
   - Garnish with additional strawberries and a dusting of powdered sugar, if desired.
6. **Serve:**
   - Serve the vegan strawberry shortcakes immediately, while the biscuits are still slightly warm and the whipped cream is fluffy.

This Vegan Strawberry Shortcake is a delightful dessert that celebrates the sweetness of fresh strawberries with tender biscuits and creamy coconut whipped cream. Enjoy it as a refreshing treat during strawberry season or any time you crave a delicious dessert!

## Pineapple Coconut Nice Cream

### Ingredients:

- 4 cups frozen pineapple chunks
- 1 can (14 oz) coconut milk (full-fat), chilled in the refrigerator overnight
- 2-4 tbsp maple syrup or agave syrup (adjust to taste)
- 1 tsp vanilla extract
- Optional toppings: shredded coconut, fresh pineapple chunks, mint leaves

### Instructions:

1. **Prepare the Coconut Milk:**
   - Place the can of coconut milk in the refrigerator overnight to allow the coconut cream to solidify at the top.
2. **Make the Nice Cream:**
   - In a food processor or high-speed blender, add the frozen pineapple chunks, chilled coconut cream (scoop out the solid cream part from the can of coconut milk), maple syrup (or agave syrup), and vanilla extract.
   - Blend until smooth and creamy, scraping down the sides as needed. If the mixture is too thick to blend, you can add a splash of non-dairy milk (such as almond milk or coconut milk) to help it blend smoothly.
3. **Adjust Sweetness:**
   - Taste the nice cream and adjust sweetness if needed by adding more maple syrup or agave syrup, blending briefly to combine.
4. **Serve:**
   - Serve the pineapple coconut nice cream immediately for a soft-serve consistency, or transfer it to a container and freeze for 1-2 hours for a firmer texture.
5. **Optional Toppings:**
   - Garnish with shredded coconut, fresh pineapple chunks, or mint leaves before serving, if desired.
6. **Enjoy:**
   - Enjoy this creamy and tropical vegan pineapple coconut nice cream as a refreshing dessert or snack!

This recipe is perfect for hot summer days or anytime you're craving a tropical treat. It's naturally sweetened with the flavors of pineapple and coconut, making it a healthier alternative to traditional ice cream.

# Chocolate Avocado Cookies

**Ingredients:**

- 1 ripe avocado
- 1/2 cup coconut sugar or brown sugar
- 1/4 cup maple syrup or agave syrup
- 1/4 cup coconut oil, melted
- 1 tsp vanilla extract
- 1/2 cup cocoa powder
- 1 cup all-purpose flour (or gluten-free flour blend)
- 1/2 tsp baking powder
- 1/4 tsp salt
- 1/2 cup dairy-free chocolate chips

**Instructions:**

1. **Preheat** your oven to 350°F (175°C). Line a baking sheet with parchment paper.
2. **Prepare the Avocado:**
   - Scoop out the flesh of the ripe avocado and mash it well in a bowl until smooth.
3. **Mix Wet Ingredients:**
   - To the mashed avocado, add coconut sugar (or brown sugar), maple syrup (or agave syrup), melted coconut oil, and vanilla extract. Mix until well combined and smooth.
4. **Add Dry Ingredients:**
   - Sift in cocoa powder, all-purpose flour (or gluten-free flour blend), baking powder, and salt into the bowl with the wet ingredients. Mix until a soft dough forms.
   - Fold in dairy-free chocolate chips until evenly distributed in the dough.
5. **Form Cookies:**
   - Scoop about 1 tablespoon of dough and roll it into a ball. Place it on the prepared baking sheet. Repeat with the remaining dough, spacing the cookies about 2 inches apart.
6. **Flatten (Optional):**
   - Optionally, you can gently flatten each cookie with the palm of your hand or the back of a spoon for a more cookie-like shape.
7. **Bake:**
   - Bake in the preheated oven for 10-12 minutes, or until the cookies are set. They will be soft when you remove them from the oven but will firm up as they cool.
8. **Cool and Serve:**
   - Remove from the oven and let the cookies cool on the baking sheet for 5 minutes before transferring them to a wire rack to cool completely.
9. **Enjoy:**
   - Once cooled, enjoy these vegan chocolate avocado cookies with a glass of almond milk or your favorite dairy-free beverage!

These cookies are decadent and fudgy, with a hint of avocado that adds moisture and richness. They are perfect for chocolate lovers and a great way to sneak in some healthy fats from avocado.

**Vanilla Bean Panna Cotta**

**Ingredients:**

- 1 can (14 oz) full-fat coconut milk
- 1/2 cup unsweetened almond milk (or other non-dairy milk)
- 1/4 cup maple syrup or agave syrup
- 1 vanilla bean pod (or 1 tsp vanilla extract)
- 1 tbsp agar agar flakes or powder
- Fresh berries or fruit, for garnish (optional)

**Instructions:**

1. **Prepare the Vanilla Bean:**
    - If using a vanilla bean pod, slice it lengthwise and scrape out the seeds using the back of a knife.
2. **Combine Ingredients:**
    - In a saucepan, combine the full-fat coconut milk, unsweetened almond milk, maple syrup (or agave syrup), and the scraped vanilla bean seeds (or vanilla extract if using).
    - Stir well to combine.
3. **Heat and Simmer:**
    - Sprinkle the agar agar flakes or powder evenly over the mixture in the saucepan. Let it sit for 5 minutes to allow the agar agar to soften.
    - Place the saucepan over medium heat and bring the mixture to a gentle simmer, stirring occasionally to dissolve the agar agar completely. This usually takes about 5-7 minutes.
4. **Remove from Heat:**
    - Once the mixture has simmered and the agar agar is fully dissolved, remove the saucepan from heat. Taste and adjust sweetness if needed by adding more maple syrup or agave syrup.
5. **Pour into Molds:**
    - Pour the mixture into individual ramekins or molds. Allow it to cool at room temperature for 15-20 minutes.
6. **Chill:**
    - Cover each ramekin or mold with plastic wrap or foil and refrigerate for at least 4 hours, or until the panna cotta is set and firm.
7. **Serve:**
    - To serve, carefully run a knife around the edge of each panna cotta and invert onto a serving plate. Alternatively, serve directly in the ramekins or molds.
    - Garnish with fresh berries or fruit, if desired.
8. **Enjoy:**
    - Serve and enjoy this creamy and vegan-friendly Vanilla Bean Panna Cotta as a delightful dessert!

This recipe captures the essence of traditional panna cotta with a vegan twist using coconut milk and agar agar to achieve a creamy texture without dairy. It's a perfect dessert for special occasions or anytime you crave a luxurious treat.

## Apple Cinnamon Rolls

**Ingredients:**

**For the Dough:**

- 1 cup unsweetened almond milk (or other non-dairy milk)
- 1/4 cup vegan butter, melted
- 1/4 cup granulated sugar
- 2 1/4 tsp (1 packet) active dry yeast
- 3 cups all-purpose flour (plus extra for dusting)
- 1/2 tsp salt

**For the Apple Filling:**

- 2 medium apples, peeled, cored, and finely chopped
- 1/4 cup brown sugar
- 1 tsp ground cinnamon
- 1/4 tsp ground nutmeg
- 2 tbsp vegan butter, melted

**For the Cinnamon Glaze:**

- 1 cup powdered sugar
- 1-2 tbsp almond milk (or other non-dairy milk)
- 1/2 tsp vanilla extract
- 1/2 tsp ground cinnamon

**Instructions:**

1. **Prepare the Dough:**
    - In a small saucepan, warm the almond milk until it is lukewarm (about 110°F or 45°C). Transfer to a large mixing bowl.
    - Stir in the melted vegan butter and granulated sugar until well combined.
    - Sprinkle the yeast over the mixture and let it sit for about 5-10 minutes, until foamy.
2. **Mix the Dough:**
    - Add 2 cups of flour and salt to the yeast mixture. Stir until well combined.
    - Gradually add the remaining 1 cup of flour, mixing until the dough comes together and pulls away from the sides of the bowl.
3. **Knead the Dough:**
    - Turn the dough out onto a lightly floured surface. Knead for about 5-7 minutes, adding more flour as needed, until the dough is smooth and elastic.
4. **First Rise:**
    - Place the dough in a lightly greased bowl and cover with a clean kitchen towel. Let it rise in a warm place for about 1-1.5 hours, or until doubled in size.

5. **Prepare the Apple Filling:**
   - In a small bowl, combine the chopped apples, brown sugar, ground cinnamon, and ground nutmeg. Set aside.
6. **Roll out the Dough:**
   - Punch down the risen dough and roll it out on a lightly floured surface into a large rectangle, about 12x18 inches.
7. **Add the Filling:**
   - Brush the melted vegan butter over the rolled-out dough.
   - Spread the apple filling evenly over the dough, leaving a small border around the edges.
8. **Roll up the Dough:**
   - Starting from one of the longer edges, tightly roll up the dough into a log. Pinch the seam to seal.
9. **Cut the Rolls:**
   - Using a sharp knife or dental floss, cut the dough into 12 equal-sized rolls. Place them in a greased 9x13 inch baking dish, leaving a little space between each roll.
10. **Second Rise:**
    - Cover the baking dish with a kitchen towel and let the rolls rise in a warm place for another 30-45 minutes, until they are puffy.
11. **Bake:**
    - Preheat your oven to 375°F (190°C). Bake the rolls for 25-30 minutes, or until they are golden brown.
12. **Make the Cinnamon Glaze:**
    - While the rolls are baking, prepare the cinnamon glaze. In a small bowl, whisk together powdered sugar, almond milk (start with 1 tbsp and add more as needed for desired consistency), vanilla extract, and ground cinnamon until smooth.
13. **Glaze the Rolls:**
    - Remove the rolls from the oven and let them cool in the pan for a few minutes.
    - Drizzle the cinnamon glaze over the warm rolls.
14. **Serve:**
    - Serve the Vegan Apple Cinnamon Rolls warm. Enjoy the delicious combination of soft dough, sweet apple filling, and aromatic cinnamon!

These Vegan Apple Cinnamon Rolls are perfect for breakfast, brunch, or as a comforting dessert. They're sure to be a hit with family and friends, offering a vegan twist on a classic favorite.

**Vegan Lemon Bars**

**Ingredients:**

**For the Crust:**

- 1 cup all-purpose flour
- 1/4 cup powdered sugar
- 1/2 cup vegan butter or margarine, cold and cubed

**For the Lemon Filling:**

- 1 cup granulated sugar
- 1/4 cup cornstarch
- 1/4 tsp salt
- 1 cup full-fat coconut milk (from a can)
- 3/4 cup fresh lemon juice (about 4-5 lemons)
- Zest of 1-2 lemons (optional, for extra lemon flavor)
- Powdered sugar, for dusting (optional)

**Instructions:**

1. **Preheat** your oven to 350°F (175°C). Line an 8x8 inch baking dish with parchment paper, leaving some overhang for easy removal.
2. **Make the Crust:**
    - In a food processor, combine the flour and powdered sugar. Pulse a few times to mix.
    - Add the cold cubed vegan butter and pulse until the mixture resembles coarse crumbs and starts to come together.
    - Press the mixture evenly into the bottom of the prepared baking dish.
3. **Bake the Crust:**
    - Bake the crust in the preheated oven for 15-18 minutes, or until lightly golden. Remove from the oven and set aside to cool slightly.
4. **Prepare the Lemon Filling:**
    - In a medium saucepan, whisk together the granulated sugar, cornstarch, and salt.
    - Gradually whisk in the coconut milk and lemon juice until smooth.
    - Place the saucepan over medium heat and cook, stirring constantly, until the mixture thickens and comes to a gentle boil. This usually takes about 5-7 minutes.
    - Remove from heat and stir in the lemon zest, if using.
5. **Assemble and Bake:**
    - Pour the lemon filling over the baked crust, spreading it out evenly with a spatula.
    - Return the baking dish to the oven and bake for an additional 15-20 minutes, or until the filling is set and the edges are lightly golden.

6. **Cool and Chill:**
   - Remove the lemon bars from the oven and let them cool completely in the baking dish on a wire rack.
   - Once cooled, refrigerate the bars for at least 2 hours, or until chilled and firm.
7. **Serve:**
   - Lift the bars out of the baking dish using the parchment paper overhang. Dust with powdered sugar, if desired, and cut into squares.
8. **Enjoy:**
   - Serve these delicious Vegan Lemon Bars chilled. They are tangy, sweet, and perfect for a refreshing dessert!

These Vegan Lemon Bars are a wonderful combination of a buttery crust and a silky smooth lemon filling. They're sure to be a hit with anyone who loves citrusy desserts!

# Hazelnut Chocolate Brownies

**Ingredients:**

- 1 cup all-purpose flour
- 1/2 cup cocoa powder
- 1 tsp baking powder
- 1/2 tsp salt
- 1/2 cup vegan butter or coconut oil, melted
- 1 cup granulated sugar
- 1/2 cup non-dairy milk (such as almond milk or soy milk)
- 1 tsp vanilla extract
- 1/2 cup chopped hazelnuts
- 1/2 cup dairy-free chocolate chips or chunks

**Instructions:**

1. **Preheat** your oven to 350°F (175°C). Grease or line an 8x8 inch baking dish with parchment paper.
2. **Mix Dry Ingredients:**
    - In a medium bowl, whisk together the all-purpose flour, cocoa powder, baking powder, and salt until well combined.
3. **Prepare Wet Ingredients:**
    - In a separate large bowl, whisk together the melted vegan butter or coconut oil and granulated sugar until smooth.
    - Add the non-dairy milk and vanilla extract, and whisk until combined.
4. **Combine and Fold:**
    - Gradually add the dry ingredients to the wet ingredients, stirring until just combined.
    - Fold in the chopped hazelnuts and dairy-free chocolate chips or chunks until evenly distributed in the batter.
5. **Bake:**
    - Pour the batter into the prepared baking dish and spread it out evenly with a spatula.
    - Bake in the preheated oven for 25-30 minutes, or until a toothpick inserted into the center comes out with a few moist crumbs.
6. **Cool and Serve:**
    - Allow the brownies to cool completely in the baking dish on a wire rack before slicing into squares.
7. **Enjoy:**
    - Serve these delicious Vegan Hazelnut Chocolate Brownies at room temperature. They are rich, fudgy, and packed with chocolate and hazelnut flavors!

These brownies are perfect for any occasion, whether you're celebrating a special event or simply indulging in a sweet treat. The combination of hazelnuts and chocolate creates a delightful flavor profile that will satisfy any chocolate lover's cravings.

**Pecan Pie**

**Ingredients:**

**For the Pie Crust:**

- 1 1/4 cups all-purpose flour
- 1/4 tsp salt
- 1/2 cup vegan butter, cold and cubed
- 2-4 tbsp ice water

**For the Pecan Filling:**

- 1 cup chopped pecans
- 1 cup full-fat coconut milk (from a can)
- 1/2 cup brown sugar
- 1/4 cup maple syrup or agave syrup
- 2 tbsp cornstarch
- 1 tsp vanilla extract
- 1/4 tsp salt

**Instructions:**

1. **Prepare the Pie Crust:**
    - In a food processor, combine the all-purpose flour and salt. Add the cold cubed vegan butter and pulse until the mixture resembles coarse crumbs.
    - Gradually add ice water, 1 tablespoon at a time, and pulse until the dough starts to come together. You may not need all the water.
    - Turn the dough out onto a lightly floured surface and knead it gently into a ball. Flatten into a disc, wrap in plastic wrap, and refrigerate for at least 30 minutes.
2. **Preheat** your oven to 350°F (175°C).
3. **Roll out the Pie Crust:**
    - On a lightly floured surface, roll out the chilled pie dough into a circle about 12 inches in diameter. Carefully transfer the rolled-out dough to a 9-inch pie dish. Trim any excess dough hanging over the edge and crimp the edges as desired.
4. **Prepare the Pecan Filling:**
    - In a medium bowl, whisk together the coconut milk, brown sugar, maple syrup (or agave syrup), cornstarch, vanilla extract, and salt until smooth.
    - Stir in the chopped pecans until evenly coated.
5. **Assemble and Bake:**
    - Pour the pecan filling into the prepared pie crust, spreading it out evenly.
    - Cover the edges of the pie crust with aluminum foil or a pie crust shield to prevent them from over-browning.
    - Bake in the preheated oven for 40-45 minutes, or until the filling is set and the crust is golden brown.

6. **Cool and Serve:**
   - Allow the pecan pie to cool completely on a wire rack before slicing and serving.
7. **Enjoy:**
   - Serve slices of this delicious Vegan Pecan Pie at room temperature or slightly warmed, optionally with a dollop of dairy-free whipped cream or a scoop of vegan ice cream.

This Vegan Pecan Pie is a wonderful dessert that captures the classic flavors and textures of traditional pecan pie, without any animal products. It's perfect for holiday gatherings or any time you're craving a sweet and nutty treat!

# Key Lime Pie

## Ingredients:

### For the Graham Cracker Crust:

- 1 1/2 cups graham cracker crumbs (about 10-12 sheets)
- 1/4 cup granulated sugar
- 1/2 cup vegan butter, melted

### For the Key Lime Filling:

- 1 can (14 oz) full-fat coconut milk (chilled in the refrigerator overnight)
- 1/2 cup fresh key lime juice (about 15-20 key limes)
- Zest of 2 key limes (optional, for extra flavor)
- 1/2 cup powdered sugar (adjust to taste)
- 1 tsp vanilla extract

### For Garnish (optional):

- Lime zest
- Sliced limes
- Vegan whipped cream

## Instructions:

1. **Prepare the Graham Cracker Crust:**
   - Preheat your oven to 350°F (175°C).
   - In a bowl, mix together the graham cracker crumbs, granulated sugar, and melted vegan butter until well combined and the mixture resembles wet sand.
   - Press the mixture evenly into the bottom and up the sides of a 9-inch pie dish.
   - Bake the crust in the preheated oven for 10-12 minutes, or until lightly golden and fragrant. Remove from the oven and let it cool completely on a wire rack.
2. **Make the Key Lime Filling:**
   - Open the chilled can of coconut milk and scoop out the solid coconut cream that has risen to the top. Save the coconut water for another use.
   - In a bowl, whisk together the coconut cream, fresh key lime juice, lime zest (if using), powdered sugar, and vanilla extract until smooth and well combined.
   - Taste the filling and adjust sweetness if needed by adding more powdered sugar.
3. **Assemble the Key Lime Pie:**
   - Pour the key lime filling into the cooled graham cracker crust, spreading it out evenly with a spatula.
4. **Chill:**
   - Cover the pie with plastic wrap or foil and refrigerate for at least 4 hours, or until the filling is set and firm.
5. **Serve:**

- Before serving, garnish the pie with lime zest, sliced limes, or a dollop of vegan whipped cream, if desired.
6. **Enjoy:**
    - Slice and serve this refreshing Vegan Key Lime Pie chilled. It's tangy, creamy, and perfect for summer or anytime you crave a citrusy dessert!

This Vegan Key Lime Pie captures the zesty flavors of key limes with a creamy coconut milk base, all nestled in a delicious graham cracker crust. It's a delightful and satisfying dessert that's sure to be enjoyed by vegans and non-vegans alike!

**Caramelized Banana Ice Cream**

**Ingredients:**

- 4 ripe bananas, peeled and sliced
- 1/4 cup brown sugar
- 2 tbsp vegan butter or coconut oil
- 1 tsp vanilla extract
- 1 can (14 oz) full-fat coconut milk, chilled in the refrigerator overnight
- Optional: chopped nuts or dairy-free chocolate chips for garnish

**Instructions:**

1. **Caramelize the Bananas:**
    - In a skillet or frying pan, melt the vegan butter or coconut oil over medium heat.
    - Add the sliced bananas and sprinkle them with brown sugar.
    - Cook the bananas for 3-4 minutes on each side, or until they are caramelized and golden brown.
    - Remove from heat and stir in the vanilla extract. Let the caramelized bananas cool completely.
2. **Prepare the Coconut Milk:**
    - Open the chilled can of coconut milk and scoop out the solid coconut cream that has risen to the top. Save the coconut water for another use.
3. **Blend the Ice Cream:**
    - In a blender or food processor, combine the caramelized bananas (including any syrup from the pan) and the coconut cream.
    - Blend until smooth and creamy. Taste and adjust sweetness if needed by adding a bit more brown sugar or a dash of maple syrup.
4. **Chill and Freeze:**
    - Transfer the mixture into a freezer-safe container. Cover with a lid or plastic wrap directly touching the surface of the ice cream to prevent ice crystals from forming.
    - Freeze for at least 4 hours, or until the ice cream is firm and scoopable.
5. **Serve:**
    - Remove the ice cream from the freezer and let it sit at room temperature for a few minutes to soften slightly before scooping.
    - Scoop into bowls or cones, garnish with chopped nuts or dairy-free chocolate chips if desired, and enjoy!

This Vegan Caramelized Banana Ice Cream is creamy, naturally sweetened, and full of caramelized banana flavor. It's a perfect dairy-free dessert option that everyone will love, especially on warm days!

**Vegan Rice Pudding**

**Ingredients:**

- 1 cup Arborio rice (or any short-grain rice)
- 4 cups unsweetened almond milk (or any non-dairy milk)
- 1/2 cup coconut milk (full-fat, from a can)
- 1/4 cup granulated sugar (adjust to taste)
- 1/4 cup maple syrup or agave syrup
- 1 tsp vanilla extract
- 1/4 tsp ground cinnamon
- Pinch of salt
- Optional toppings: Cinnamon powder, fresh berries, chopped nuts

**Instructions:**

1. **Cook the Rice:**
   - In a large saucepan, combine the Arborio rice and almond milk over medium heat.
   - Bring to a gentle simmer, stirring occasionally to prevent sticking, for about 20-25 minutes or until the rice is tender and creamy.
2. **Add Sweeteners and Flavorings:**
   - Stir in the coconut milk, granulated sugar, maple syrup (or agave syrup), vanilla extract, ground cinnamon, and a pinch of salt.
   - Continue to simmer for another 5-10 minutes, stirring occasionally, until the mixture thickens to your desired consistency.
3. **Serve:**
   - Remove from heat and let the rice pudding cool slightly.
   - Serve warm or chilled, topped with a sprinkle of cinnamon powder, fresh berries, or chopped nuts if desired.
4. **Enjoy:**
   - Enjoy this creamy and comforting Vegan Rice Pudding as a delicious dessert or snack!

This vegan version of rice pudding is rich and creamy, thanks to the combination of almond milk and coconut milk. The sweetness can be adjusted to your preference with maple syrup, and the addition of cinnamon and vanilla enhances the flavor beautifully. It's a versatile dessert that can be enjoyed warm on cold days or chilled during warmer weather.

# Blackberry Cobbler

## Ingredients:

### For the Blackberry Filling:

- 4 cups fresh or frozen blackberries
- 1/2 cup granulated sugar
- 2 tbsp cornstarch
- 1 tbsp lemon juice
- Zest of 1 lemon (optional)
- 1/2 tsp vanilla extract

### For the Biscuit Topping:

- 1 cup all-purpose flour
- 1/4 cup granulated sugar
- 1 1/2 tsp baking powder
- 1/4 tsp salt
- 1/4 cup vegan butter, cold and cubed
- 1/3 cup non-dairy milk (such as almond milk or soy milk)
- 1 tsp vanilla extract

## Instructions:

1. **Preheat** your oven to 375°F (190°C). Lightly grease a 9x9 inch baking dish or a similar-sized baking pan.
2. **Prepare the Blackberry Filling:**
   - In a large bowl, combine the blackberries, granulated sugar, cornstarch, lemon juice, lemon zest (if using), and vanilla extract. Toss gently to coat the blackberries evenly.
3. **Transfer to Baking Dish:**
   - Pour the blackberry mixture into the prepared baking dish, spreading it out evenly.
4. **Make the Biscuit Topping:**
   - In a separate bowl, whisk together the all-purpose flour, granulated sugar, baking powder, and salt.
   - Add the cold cubed vegan butter to the flour mixture. Using a pastry cutter or your fingers, work the butter into the flour until the mixture resembles coarse crumbs.
   - In a small bowl, combine the non-dairy milk and vanilla extract. Pour the milk mixture into the flour mixture and stir until just combined. Do not overmix; the dough should be slightly sticky.
5. **Assemble and Bake:**

    - Drop spoonfuls of the biscuit dough evenly over the blackberry filling. The dough will spread out as it bakes.
6. **Bake the Cobbler:**
    - Bake in the preheated oven for 35-40 minutes, or until the topping is golden brown and the blackberry filling is bubbly.
7. **Cool and Serve:**
    - Remove the cobbler from the oven and let it cool slightly on a wire rack before serving.
8. **Enjoy:**
    - Serve warm with a scoop of dairy-free vanilla ice cream or a dollop of coconut whipped cream, if desired. Enjoy this delicious Vegan Blackberry Cobbler as a comforting dessert!

This Vegan Blackberry Cobbler is perfect for showcasing fresh or frozen blackberries and makes a wonderful treat for any occasion. The combination of juicy fruit filling and tender biscuit topping is sure to be a hit!

# Sweet Potato Pie

**Ingredients:**

**For the Crust:**

- 1 1/4 cups all-purpose flour
- 1/4 tsp salt
- 1/2 cup vegan butter, cold and cubed
- 2-4 tbsp ice water

**For the Sweet Potato Filling:**

- 2 medium sweet potatoes (about 1 lb), peeled and cubed
- 1/2 cup coconut milk (full-fat, from a can)
- 1/2 cup brown sugar
- 1/4 cup maple syrup or agave syrup
- 1 tsp vanilla extract
- 1 tsp ground cinnamon
- 1/2 tsp ground nutmeg
- 1/4 tsp ground ginger
- 1/4 tsp salt

**Instructions:**

1. **Prepare the Crust:**
   - In a food processor, combine the all-purpose flour and salt. Add the cold cubed vegan butter and pulse until the mixture resembles coarse crumbs.
   - Gradually add ice water, 1 tablespoon at a time, and pulse until the dough starts to come together. You may not need all the water.
   - Turn the dough out onto a lightly floured surface and knead it gently into a ball. Flatten into a disc, wrap in plastic wrap, and refrigerate for at least 30 minutes.
2. **Preheat** your oven to 375°F (190°C).
3. **Prepare the Sweet Potatoes:**
   - Place the cubed sweet potatoes in a pot of water. Bring to a boil and cook for 15-20 minutes, or until the sweet potatoes are tender. Drain well and let cool slightly.
   - Mash the cooked sweet potatoes until smooth. You should have about 2 cups of mashed sweet potatoes.
4. **Make the Sweet Potato Filling:**
   - In a large bowl, combine the mashed sweet potatoes, coconut milk, brown sugar, maple syrup (or agave syrup), vanilla extract, ground cinnamon, ground nutmeg, ground ginger, and salt. Mix until smooth and well combined.
5. **Assemble and Bake:**

- Roll out the chilled pie crust on a lightly floured surface into a circle about 12 inches in diameter. Carefully transfer it to a 9-inch pie dish. Trim any excess dough hanging over the edge and crimp the edges as desired.
  - Pour the sweet potato filling into the prepared pie crust, spreading it out evenly with a spatula.
6. **Bake the Pie:**
   - Bake in the preheated oven for 50-60 minutes, or until the filling is set and the crust is golden brown. If the crust edges start to brown too quickly, cover them with aluminum foil halfway through baking.
7. **Cool and Serve:**
   - Remove the pie from the oven and let it cool completely on a wire rack before slicing and serving.
8. **Enjoy:**
   - Serve slices of this delicious Vegan Sweet Potato Pie at room temperature or slightly chilled. It's creamy, spiced, and perfect for holiday gatherings or any time you crave a comforting dessert!

This Vegan Sweet Potato Pie is a delightful twist on the classic, offering a creamy filling with warm spices that complement the sweet potatoes beautifully. It's sure to be a hit with vegans and non-vegans alike!

# Pistachio Rosewater Cookies

**Ingredients:**

- 1 cup shelled pistachios
- 1 cup all-purpose flour
- 1/2 cup powdered sugar
- 1/2 cup vegan butter or coconut oil, softened
- 1-2 tbsp rosewater (adjust to taste)
- 1/2 tsp vanilla extract
- A pinch of salt
- Optional: Rose petals or chopped pistachios for garnish

**Instructions:**

1. **Prepare the Pistachios:**
   - Preheat your oven to 350°F (175°C). Spread the pistachios on a baking sheet and toast them in the oven for 8-10 minutes, or until lightly golden and fragrant. Let them cool completely.
2. **Grind the Pistachios:**
   - Once cooled, place the toasted pistachios in a food processor and pulse until finely ground. Some larger pieces are fine for texture.
3. **Make the Cookie Dough:**
   - In a large bowl, cream together the powdered sugar and vegan butter (or coconut oil) until smooth and creamy.
   - Add the ground pistachios, all-purpose flour, rosewater, vanilla extract, and a pinch of salt to the bowl. Mix until well combined and a dough forms. If the dough is too dry, add a teaspoon of water or more rosewater until it comes together.
4. **Chill the Dough:**
   - Shape the dough into a ball, wrap it in plastic wrap, and refrigerate for at least 30 minutes to firm up.
5. **Preheat** your oven to 350°F (175°C). Line a baking sheet with parchment paper.
6. **Shape the Cookies:**
   - Take tablespoons of dough and roll them into balls. Place them on the prepared baking sheet, spacing them about 2 inches apart.
7. **Bake the Cookies:**
   - Bake in the preheated oven for 12-15 minutes, or until the edges are lightly golden. The tops of the cookies should still be pale.
8. **Cool and Garnish:**
   - Let the cookies cool on the baking sheet for 5 minutes, then transfer them to a wire rack to cool completely.
9. **Optional Garnish:**
   - If desired, sprinkle the cooled cookies with rose petals or chopped pistachios for decoration.
10. **Enjoy:**

- Serve these Vegan Pistachio Rosewater Cookies with a cup of tea or coffee. They have a delicate nutty flavor with a hint of floral sweetness, making them a perfect treat for any occasion!

These cookies are a unique and delicious twist on traditional pistachio cookies, enhanced with the subtle aroma of rosewater. They're sure to impress with their flavor and lovely appearance!

## Coconut Flour Pancakes

**Ingredients:**

- 1/2 cup coconut flour
- 1/2 cup almond flour
- 1 tsp baking powder
- Pinch of salt
- 1 cup non-dairy milk (such as almond milk or coconut milk)
- 2 tbsp maple syrup or agave syrup
- 2 tbsp melted coconut oil (plus more for cooking)
- 1 tsp vanilla extract

**Instructions:**

1. **Mix Dry Ingredients:**
     - In a bowl, whisk together the coconut flour, almond flour, baking powder, and salt until well combined.
2. **Prepare Wet Ingredients:**
     - In another bowl, whisk together the non-dairy milk, maple syrup (or agave syrup), melted coconut oil, and vanilla extract until smooth.
3. **Combine Wet and Dry Ingredients:**
     - Pour the wet ingredients into the bowl with the dry ingredients. Stir until just combined. Let the batter sit for a few minutes to thicken slightly. Coconut flour absorbs a lot of liquid, so the batter may thicken as it sits.
4. **Cook the Pancakes:**
     - Heat a non-stick skillet or griddle over medium heat. Lightly grease with coconut oil.
     - Pour about 1/4 cup of batter onto the skillet for each pancake. Spread the batter slightly with the back of a spoon to form circles.
     - Cook for 2-3 minutes, or until bubbles form on the surface of the pancakes and the edges look set.
     - Carefully flip the pancakes and cook for another 1-2 minutes on the other side, until golden brown and cooked through.
5. **Serve:**
     - Serve the pancakes warm with your favorite toppings such as fresh berries, sliced bananas, maple syrup, or a dollop of dairy-free yogurt.
6. **Enjoy:**
     - Enjoy these fluffy Vegan Coconut Flour Pancakes for a delicious and nutritious breakfast or brunch!

These pancakes are not only gluten-free and vegan but also packed with coconut and almond flavors, making them a delightful and wholesome treat. Adjust the sweetness and texture to your liking by varying the amount of maple syrup and thickness of the batter.

**Chocolate Chia Seed Pudding**

**Ingredients:**

- 1/4 cup chia seeds
- 1 cup non-dairy milk (such as almond milk, coconut milk, or soy milk)
- 2 tbsp cocoa powder (unsweetened)
- 2-3 tbsp maple syrup or agave syrup (adjust to taste)
- 1/2 tsp vanilla extract
- Optional toppings: Fresh berries, sliced bananas, coconut flakes, chopped nuts

**Instructions:**

1. **Mix Ingredients:**
    - In a bowl or jar, combine the chia seeds, non-dairy milk, cocoa powder, maple syrup (or agave syrup), and vanilla extract. Stir well until the cocoa powder is fully dissolved and mixed into the liquid.
2. **Let it Set:**
    - Cover the bowl or jar and refrigerate for at least 2 hours, or preferably overnight. Chia seeds will absorb the liquid and thicken, creating a pudding-like consistency.
3. **Stir Again:**
    - After the pudding has set, give it a good stir to break up any clumps and ensure an even texture.
4. **Serve:**
    - Divide the chocolate chia seed pudding into serving bowls or jars.
5. **Top and Enjoy:**
    - Top with your favorite toppings such as fresh berries, sliced bananas, coconut flakes, or chopped nuts.
6. **Enjoy:**
    - Enjoy this Vegan Chocolate Chia Seed Pudding as a nutritious breakfast, snack, or dessert!

This pudding is rich in fiber, omega-3 fatty acids, and antioxidants from the chia seeds, while the cocoa powder adds a delicious chocolate flavor. It's a versatile recipe that you can customize with your favorite toppings and adjust the sweetness to your liking.

# Vegan Oreo Cheesecake

**Ingredients:**

**For the Oreo Crust:**

- 20 Oreo cookies (vegan-friendly)
- 1/4 cup vegan butter, melted

**For the Cheesecake Filling:**

- 2 cups raw cashews, soaked in hot water for 1 hour or in cold water overnight, then drained
- 1/2 cup coconut cream (from a can of full-fat coconut milk)
- 1/2 cup coconut oil, melted
- 1/2 cup maple syrup or agave syrup
- 1/4 cup lemon juice
- 1 tsp vanilla extract
- 10 Oreo cookies (for mixing into the filling)
- Optional: Additional Oreo cookies for decorating the top

**Instructions:**

1. **Prepare the Oreo Crust:**
    - Grease a 9-inch springform pan with vegan butter or coconut oil.
    - In a food processor, pulse the Oreo cookies (cream included) until they are finely ground.
    - Add the melted vegan butter and pulse again until well combined and the mixture resembles wet sand.
    - Press the mixture evenly into the bottom of the prepared springform pan. Use the back of a spoon or a flat-bottomed glass to compact the crust.
2. **Prepare the Cheesecake Filling:**
    - In a high-speed blender, combine the soaked and drained cashews, coconut cream, melted coconut oil, maple syrup (or agave syrup), lemon juice, and vanilla extract.
    - Blend on high until the mixture is smooth and creamy, scraping down the sides of the blender as needed to ensure everything is well incorporated.
3. **Add Oreos to Filling:**
    - Break or roughly chop 10 Oreo cookies into smaller pieces and fold them into the cheesecake filling using a spatula or spoon.
4. **Assemble and Chill:**
    - Pour the cheesecake filling over the prepared Oreo crust in the springform pan, spreading it out evenly with a spatula.
    - Tap the pan gently on the countertop to remove any air bubbles.
5. **Chill the Cheesecake:**

- Cover the cheesecake with plastic wrap or aluminum foil and refrigerate for at least 6 hours, or preferably overnight, until set.
6. **Decorate and Serve:**
    - Before serving, optionally decorate the top of the cheesecake with additional Oreo cookies.
    - Release the springform pan and slice the Vegan Oreo Cheesecake into slices.
7. **Enjoy:**
    - Serve chilled and enjoy this decadent Vegan Oreo Cheesecake as a delicious dessert!

This cheesecake is creamy, full of Oreo flavor, and completely vegan-friendly. It's perfect for special occasions or whenever you're craving a rich and indulgent treat.

# Lemon Lavender Cupcakes

**Ingredients:**

**For the Cupcakes:**

- 1 1/2 cups all-purpose flour
- 1 cup granulated sugar
- 1 tsp baking powder
- 1/2 tsp baking soda
- 1/4 tsp salt
- Zest of 1 lemon
- 1 cup non-dairy milk (such as almond milk or soy milk)
- 1/3 cup freshly squeezed lemon juice
- 1/3 cup melted coconut oil or vegetable oil
- 1 tsp vanilla extract
- 1 tbsp culinary lavender (dried or culinary lavender buds)

**For the Lemon Lavender Frosting:**

- 1/2 cup vegan butter, softened
- 2 cups powdered sugar
- 1 tbsp freshly squeezed lemon juice
- 1/2 tsp vanilla extract
- 1-2 tsp culinary lavender (finely ground)

**Instructions:**

1. **Preheat** your oven to 350°F (175°C). Line a muffin tin with cupcake liners.
2. **Prepare the Cupcake Batter:**
    - In a large mixing bowl, whisk together the flour, sugar, baking powder, baking soda, salt, and lemon zest.
    - In a separate bowl, combine the non-dairy milk, lemon juice, melted coconut oil (or vegetable oil), and vanilla extract.
    - Gradually add the wet ingredients to the dry ingredients, stirring until just combined. Be careful not to overmix.
    - Gently fold in the culinary lavender until evenly distributed in the batter.
3. **Bake the Cupcakes:**
    - Divide the batter evenly among the prepared cupcake liners, filling each about 2/3 full.
    - Bake in the preheated oven for 18-20 minutes, or until a toothpick inserted into the center of a cupcake comes out clean.
    - Remove from the oven and let the cupcakes cool in the pan for 5 minutes, then transfer them to a wire rack to cool completely.
4. **Make the Lemon Lavender Frosting:**

- In a mixing bowl, beat the softened vegan butter until creamy.
- Gradually add the powdered sugar, 1/2 cup at a time, beating well after each addition.
- Add the freshly squeezed lemon juice, vanilla extract, and finely ground culinary lavender. Beat until smooth and fluffy. Adjust the consistency with more powdered sugar if needed.

5. **Frost the Cupcakes:**
    - Once the cupcakes are completely cooled, frost them generously with the lemon lavender frosting using a piping bag or offset spatula.
6. **Garnish (Optional):**
    - Optionally, garnish each cupcake with a sprinkle of culinary lavender buds or a small lemon zest curl.
7. **Serve and Enjoy:**
    - Serve these Vegan Lemon Lavender Cupcakes immediately, or store them in an airtight container in the refrigerator for up to 3 days. Enjoy the unique blend of lemon and lavender flavors in every bite!

These cupcakes are perfect for special occasions or as a delightful treat any day of the week. The combination of citrusy lemon and aromatic lavender creates a beautifully balanced flavor profile that's sure to impress!

**Almond Flour Blueberry Scones**

**Ingredients:**

- 2 cups almond flour
- 1/4 cup coconut flour
- 1/4 cup tapioca flour (or arrowroot flour)
- 1/4 cup granulated sugar (or coconut sugar)
- 1 tsp baking powder
- 1/4 tsp baking soda
- 1/4 tsp salt
- 1/4 cup coconut oil, melted
- 1/4 cup non-dairy milk (such as almond milk or oat milk)
- 1 tsp vanilla extract
- 1/2 cup fresh or frozen blueberries
- Optional: Lemon zest or almond extract for extra flavor

**Instructions:**

1. **Preheat** your oven to 350°F (175°C). Line a baking sheet with parchment paper.
2. **Mix Dry Ingredients:**
    - In a large bowl, whisk together the almond flour, coconut flour, tapioca flour, sugar, baking powder, baking soda, and salt.
3. **Add Wet Ingredients:**
    - Add the melted coconut oil, non-dairy milk, and vanilla extract to the dry ingredients. Stir until well combined. The dough will be crumbly.
4. **Fold in Blueberries:**
    - Gently fold in the blueberries until evenly distributed throughout the dough. Be careful not to overmix to avoid crushing the blueberries.
5. **Shape the Scones:**
    - Transfer the dough onto the prepared baking sheet. Form the dough into a circle about 1 inch thick.
    - Use a knife or bench scraper to cut the circle into 8 triangular scones.
6. **Bake the Scones:**
    - Bake in the preheated oven for 18-20 minutes, or until the scones are lightly golden brown around the edges.
7. **Cool and Serve:**
    - Remove from the oven and let the scones cool on the baking sheet for 5 minutes, then transfer them to a wire rack to cool completely.
8. **Enjoy:**
    - Serve these Vegan Almond Flour Blueberry Scones warm or at room temperature. They're perfect on their own or with a dollop of dairy-free yogurt and a drizzle of maple syrup.

These scones are not only gluten-free and vegan but also packed with almond flour goodness and juicy blueberries. They make a delicious breakfast or snack that everyone will enjoy!

## Chocolate Peanut Butter Fudge

**Ingredients:**

- 1 cup creamy peanut butter (unsweetened)
- 1/2 cup coconut oil, melted
- 1/4 cup cocoa powder (unsweetened)
- 1/4 cup maple syrup or agave syrup (adjust to taste)
- 1 tsp vanilla extract
- A pinch of salt

**Instructions:**

1. **Prepare the Fudge Base:**
   - In a microwave-safe bowl or on the stove, melt the coconut oil until it's completely liquid.
   - In a separate bowl, combine the creamy peanut butter, melted coconut oil, cocoa powder, maple syrup (or agave syrup), vanilla extract, and a pinch of salt. Mix well until smooth and creamy.
2. **Pour into a Pan:**
   - Line a square baking dish or a container with parchment paper for easy removal later. Make sure the parchment paper hangs over the edges for easy lifting.
   - Pour the fudge mixture into the prepared dish, spreading it out evenly with a spatula.
3. **Chill:**
   - Place the dish in the refrigerator and chill for at least 2-3 hours, or until the fudge is firm and set.
4. **Slice and Serve:**
   - Once the fudge is completely chilled and firm, remove it from the refrigerator and lift it out of the dish using the parchment paper.
   - Cut the fudge into squares or rectangles using a sharp knife.
5. **Enjoy:**
   - Serve and enjoy this delicious Vegan Chocolate Peanut Butter Fudge as a sweet treat or dessert!

This fudge is smooth, creamy, and combines the rich flavors of chocolate and peanut butter perfectly. It's a delightful vegan-friendly dessert that's easy to make and sure to satisfy any sweet tooth!

# Mango Coconut Rice Pudding

## Ingredients:

- 1 cup arborio rice (or any short-grain rice)
- 1 can (13.5 oz) full-fat coconut milk
- 2 cups water
- 1/4 cup granulated sugar (adjust to taste)
- 1/2 tsp vanilla extract
- 1 ripe mango, peeled and diced (plus extra for garnish)
- Pinch of salt
- Optional toppings: Toasted coconut flakes, chopped nuts, additional diced mango

## Instructions:

1. **Cook the Rice:**
   - In a large saucepan, combine the arborio rice, coconut milk, water, sugar, vanilla extract, and a pinch of salt.
   - Bring to a boil over medium-high heat, then reduce the heat to low. Simmer uncovered, stirring occasionally, for about 25-30 minutes, or until the rice is tender and the mixture is thick and creamy.
2. **Add Mango:**
   - Stir in the diced mango during the last 5 minutes of cooking. This allows the mango to soften slightly and infuse its flavor into the rice pudding.
3. **Cool and Serve:**
   - Remove the rice pudding from the heat and let it cool slightly.
4. **Chill:**
   - Transfer the rice pudding to a bowl or individual serving dishes. Cover with plastic wrap directly on the surface to prevent a skin from forming.
   - Chill in the refrigerator for at least 1-2 hours, or until completely chilled.
5. **Garnish and Serve:**
   - Before serving, garnish the mango coconut rice pudding with additional diced mango, toasted coconut flakes, and chopped nuts if desired.
6. **Enjoy:**
   - Serve chilled and enjoy this refreshing Vegan Mango Coconut Rice Pudding as a delightful dessert or snack!

This rice pudding is creamy, fragrant with coconut milk, and has the sweetness and tanginess from the fresh mango. It's a perfect dessert to enjoy during warm weather or anytime you crave a tropical treat!

**Raspberry Chocolate Chip Cookies**

**Ingredients:**

- 1/2 cup vegan butter, softened
- 1/2 cup granulated sugar
- 1/4 cup brown sugar
- 1 tsp vanilla extract
- 1 1/2 cups all-purpose flour
- 1/2 tsp baking soda
- 1/4 tsp salt
- 1/2 cup dairy-free chocolate chips
- 1/2 cup fresh raspberries, chopped

**Instructions:**

1. **Preheat** your oven to 350°F (175°C). Line a baking sheet with parchment paper.
2. **Cream the Butter and Sugars:**
   - In a mixing bowl, cream together the softened vegan butter, granulated sugar, brown sugar, and vanilla extract until smooth and creamy.
3. **Mix Dry Ingredients:**
   - In a separate bowl, whisk together the all-purpose flour, baking soda, and salt.
4. **Combine Wet and Dry Ingredients:**
   - Gradually add the dry ingredients to the creamed butter and sugar mixture, mixing until just combined.
5. **Fold in Additions:**
   - Gently fold in the dairy-free chocolate chips and chopped raspberries until evenly distributed throughout the cookie dough.
6. **Shape the Cookies:**
   - Drop spoonfuls of cookie dough onto the prepared baking sheet, spacing them about 2 inches apart.
7. **Bake the Cookies:**
   - Bake in the preheated oven for 10-12 minutes, or until the edges are lightly golden.
8. **Cool and Serve:**
   - Remove from the oven and let the cookies cool on the baking sheet for 5 minutes, then transfer them to a wire rack to cool completely.
9. **Enjoy:**
   - Serve these Vegan Raspberry Chocolate Chip Cookies warm or at room temperature. They're perfect for a sweet snack or dessert!

These cookies combine the classic flavors of chocolate and raspberries in a vegan-friendly treat that's sure to please. Enjoy the burst of raspberry freshness and the richness of chocolate chips in every bite!

**Vegan Snickerdoodles**

**Ingredients:**

- 1/2 cup vegan butter, softened
- 3/4 cup granulated sugar
- 1/4 cup unsweetened applesauce
- 1 tsp vanilla extract
- 1 3/4 cups all-purpose flour
- 1/2 tsp baking soda
- 1/4 tsp cream of tartar
- 1/4 tsp salt

**For Rolling:**

- 1/4 cup granulated sugar
- 1 tbsp ground cinnamon

**Instructions:**

1. **Preheat** your oven to 350°F (175°C). Line a baking sheet with parchment paper.
2. **Cream Butter and Sugar:**
   - In a mixing bowl, cream together the softened vegan butter and granulated sugar until light and fluffy.
3. **Add Applesauce and Vanilla:**
   - Mix in the unsweetened applesauce and vanilla extract until well combined.
4. **Combine Dry Ingredients:**
   - In a separate bowl, whisk together the all-purpose flour, baking soda, cream of tartar, and salt.
5. **Combine Wet and Dry Mixtures:**
   - Gradually add the dry ingredients to the wet ingredients, mixing until a dough forms. If the dough is too sticky, refrigerate it for 15-30 minutes.
6. **Prepare Cinnamon-Sugar Coating:**
   - In a small bowl, mix together the granulated sugar and ground cinnamon for rolling.
7. **Shape the Cookies:**
   - Roll tablespoon-sized balls of dough between your palms, then roll each ball in the cinnamon-sugar mixture until coated evenly.
8. **Bake the Cookies:**
   - Place the coated dough balls onto the prepared baking sheet, spacing them about 2 inches apart.
   - Flatten each dough ball slightly with the bottom of a glass or your fingers.
9. **Bake:**
   - Bake in the preheated oven for 10-12 minutes, or until the edges are lightly golden.

10. **Cool and Serve:**
    - Remove from the oven and let the cookies cool on the baking sheet for 5 minutes, then transfer them to a wire rack to cool completely.
11. **Enjoy:**
    - Serve these Vegan Snickerdoodles at room temperature. They're perfect with a glass of non-dairy milk or as a sweet treat any time of day!

These Vegan Snickerdoodles are soft on the inside with a slightly crispy edge, coated in a delicious cinnamon-sugar mixture. They're sure to be a hit with vegans and non-vegans alike!

**Pumpkin Spice Donuts**

**Ingredients:**

**For the Donuts:**

- 1 cup all-purpose flour
- 1/2 cup granulated sugar
- 1 tsp baking powder
- 1/2 tsp baking soda
- 1/4 tsp salt
- 1 tsp ground cinnamon
- 1/2 tsp ground nutmeg
- 1/4 tsp ground ginger
- 1/4 tsp ground cloves
- 1/2 cup pumpkin puree
- 1/4 cup unsweetened applesauce
- 1/4 cup non-dairy milk (such as almond milk or soy milk)
- 2 tbsp melted coconut oil or vegetable oil
- 1 tsp vanilla extract

**For the Cinnamon Sugar Coating:**

- 1/2 cup granulated sugar
- 1 tsp ground cinnamon
- 2-3 tbsp melted vegan butter or coconut oil (for brushing)

**Instructions:**

1. **Preheat** your oven to 350°F (175°C). Lightly grease a donut pan with oil or non-stick cooking spray.
2. **Prepare the Donut Batter:**
    - In a large bowl, whisk together the flour, sugar, baking powder, baking soda, salt, cinnamon, nutmeg, ginger, and cloves until well combined.
    - In another bowl, mix together the pumpkin puree, applesauce, non-dairy milk, melted coconut oil (or vegetable oil), and vanilla extract until smooth.
    - Pour the wet ingredients into the dry ingredients and stir until just combined. Be careful not to overmix.
3. **Fill the Donut Pan:**
    - Spoon the batter into a piping bag or a large zip-top bag with a corner snipped off. Pipe the batter into the prepared donut pan, filling each cavity about 2/3 full.
4. **Bake the Donuts:**
    - Bake in the preheated oven for 12-14 minutes, or until a toothpick inserted into the donuts comes out clean.
5. **Coat the Donuts:**

- While the donuts are baking, prepare the cinnamon sugar coating. In a shallow bowl, mix together the granulated sugar and ground cinnamon.
- Once the donuts are baked and still warm, brush each donut with melted vegan butter or coconut oil, then immediately dip them into the cinnamon sugar mixture, coating all sides.

6. **Serve and Enjoy:**
    - Serve these Vegan Pumpkin Spice Donuts warm or at room temperature. They're best enjoyed fresh on the same day they are made!

These donuts are moist, flavorful, and full of warm spices that complement the pumpkin perfectly. They're a wonderful treat for breakfast or dessert, especially during the fall season!

**Orange Cardamom Cake**

**Ingredients:**

**For the Cake:**

- 1 1/2 cups all-purpose flour
- 1 cup granulated sugar
- 1 tsp baking powder
- 1/2 tsp baking soda
- 1/4 tsp salt
- 1/2 tsp ground cardamom
- Zest of 1 orange
- 3/4 cup freshly squeezed orange juice
- 1/3 cup vegetable oil
- 1 tsp vanilla extract
- 1 tbsp apple cider vinegar

**For the Orange Glaze:**

- 1 cup powdered sugar
- 2-3 tbsp freshly squeezed orange juice

**Instructions:**

1. **Preheat** your oven to 350°F (175°C). Grease and flour a 9-inch round cake pan or line it with parchment paper.
2. **Prepare the Dry Ingredients:**
   - In a large bowl, whisk together the all-purpose flour, granulated sugar, baking powder, baking soda, salt, ground cardamom, and orange zest until well combined.
3. **Mix Wet Ingredients:**
   - In another bowl, mix together the freshly squeezed orange juice, vegetable oil, vanilla extract, and apple cider vinegar.
4. **Combine Wet and Dry Mixtures:**
   - Gradually add the wet ingredients to the dry ingredients, stirring until just combined and no lumps remain. Be careful not to overmix.
5. **Bake the Cake:**
   - Pour the batter into the prepared cake pan and spread it out evenly with a spatula.
   - Bake in the preheated oven for 30-35 minutes, or until a toothpick inserted into the center comes out clean.
6. **Cool the Cake:**
   - Remove the cake from the oven and let it cool in the pan for 10 minutes. Then, transfer it to a wire rack to cool completely.

7. **Prepare the Orange Glaze:**
   - In a small bowl, whisk together the powdered sugar and freshly squeezed orange juice until smooth and no lumps remain.
8. **Glaze the Cake:**
   - Once the cake has cooled completely, drizzle the orange glaze over the top of the cake. You can use a spoon to spread the glaze evenly over the cake.
9. **Slice and Serve:**
   - Slice the Vegan Orange Cardamom Cake and serve it as a delightful dessert or snack with a cup of tea or coffee.

This cake is moist, aromatic, and bursting with the fresh flavors of orange and cardamom. It's perfect for any occasion and is sure to impress with its unique blend of citrus and spice!

# Banana Nut Bread

## Ingredients:

- 3 ripe bananas, mashed
- 1/3 cup melted coconut oil or vegetable oil
- 1/2 cup coconut sugar or brown sugar
- 1/4 cup non-dairy milk (such as almond milk or soy milk)
- 1 tsp vanilla extract
- 1 3/4 cups all-purpose flour
- 1 tsp baking powder
- 1/2 tsp baking soda
- 1/2 tsp salt
- 1/2 tsp ground cinnamon
- 1/2 cup chopped walnuts or pecans (plus extra for topping, optional)

## Instructions:

1. **Preheat** your oven to 350°F (175°C). Grease a 9x5-inch loaf pan or line it with parchment paper.
2. **Prepare Wet Ingredients:**
   - In a large mixing bowl, combine the mashed bananas, melted coconut oil (or vegetable oil), coconut sugar (or brown sugar), non-dairy milk, and vanilla extract. Mix well until smooth.
3. **Mix Dry Ingredients:**
   - In a separate bowl, whisk together the all-purpose flour, baking powder, baking soda, salt, and ground cinnamon.
4. **Combine Wet and Dry Ingredients:**
   - Gradually add the dry ingredients to the wet ingredients, stirring until just combined and no flour pockets remain. Be careful not to overmix.
5. **Fold in Nuts:**
   - Gently fold in the chopped walnuts or pecans until evenly distributed throughout the batter.
6. **Bake the Bread:**
   - Pour the batter into the prepared loaf pan, spreading it out evenly with a spatula.
   - Optional: Sprinkle extra chopped nuts on top of the batter for a decorative touch.
   - Bake in the preheated oven for 55-65 minutes, or until a toothpick inserted into the center comes out clean.
7. **Cool and Serve:**
   - Remove the banana nut bread from the oven and let it cool in the pan for 10 minutes. Then, transfer it to a wire rack to cool completely before slicing.
8. **Enjoy:**
   - Slice the Vegan Banana Nut Bread and enjoy it warm or at room temperature. It's perfect for breakfast, as a snack, or as a comforting dessert!

This banana nut bread is moist, flavorful, and filled with the natural sweetness of ripe bananas and crunch from the nuts. It's a vegan-friendly version of a classic favorite that everyone will love!

# Berry Crumble Bars

## Ingredients:

### For the Crust and Crumble:

- 1 1/2 cups rolled oats (gluten-free if needed)
- 1 cup all-purpose flour (or oat flour for gluten-free option)
- 1/2 cup coconut sugar (or brown sugar)
- 1/2 tsp baking powder
- 1/4 tsp salt
- 1/2 cup coconut oil, melted (or vegan butter)

### For the Berry Filling:

- 3 cups mixed berries (fresh or frozen), such as raspberries, blueberries, and strawberries
- 1/4 cup coconut sugar (or granulated sugar)
- 1 tbsp cornstarch or arrowroot powder
- 1 tbsp lemon juice
- Zest of 1 lemon

## Instructions:

1. **Preheat** your oven to 350°F (175°C). Grease or line an 8x8-inch baking dish with parchment paper.
2. **Make the Crust and Crumble:**
    - In a large bowl, combine rolled oats, all-purpose flour, coconut sugar, baking powder, and salt.
    - Add melted coconut oil (or vegan butter) and mix until the mixture resembles coarse crumbs and holds together when pressed. Reserve about 1 cup of this mixture for the crumble topping.
3. **Prepare the Berry Filling:**
    - In another bowl, toss together the mixed berries, coconut sugar, cornstarch (or arrowroot powder), lemon juice, and lemon zest until well combined.
4. **Assemble the Bars:**
    - Press the remaining oat mixture firmly and evenly into the bottom of the prepared baking dish to form the crust.
    - Spread the berry filling evenly over the crust.
    - Sprinkle the reserved oat mixture evenly over the berry filling to form the crumble topping.
5. **Bake the Bars:**
    - Bake in the preheated oven for 35-40 minutes, or until the top is golden brown and the berry filling is bubbling around the edges.
6. **Cool and Serve:**

- Remove from the oven and let it cool completely in the pan on a wire rack.
- Once cooled, lift the bars out of the pan using the parchment paper overhang. Cut into squares or bars.

7. **Enjoy:**
    - Serve these Vegan Berry Crumble Bars as a delightful dessert or snack. They can be enjoyed warm or at room temperature!

These berry crumble bars are bursting with fruity flavors and have a crunchy oat crust and crumble topping. They're perfect for using seasonal berries and are sure to be a hit with vegans and non-vegans alike!

**Gingerbread Cookies**

**Ingredients:**

**For the Cookies:**

- 3 cups all-purpose flour
- 1 tsp baking soda
- 2 tsp ground ginger
- 1 tsp ground cinnamon
- 1/2 tsp ground cloves
- 1/2 tsp ground nutmeg
- 1/2 tsp salt
- 3/4 cup vegan butter, softened
- 3/4 cup brown sugar, packed
- 1/4 cup molasses
- 1 flax egg (1 tbsp ground flaxseed meal + 3 tbsp water)
- 1 tsp vanilla extract

**For the Icing (Optional):**

- 1 cup powdered sugar
- 1-2 tbsp non-dairy milk (such as almond milk or soy milk)
- Food coloring (optional)

**Instructions:**

1. **Prepare the Flax Egg:**
    - In a small bowl, mix together 1 tbsp of ground flaxseed meal with 3 tbsp of water. Let it sit for 5-10 minutes to thicken.
2. **Preheat** your oven to 350°F (175°C). Line a baking sheet with parchment paper.
3. **Mix Dry Ingredients:**
    - In a medium bowl, whisk together the all-purpose flour, baking soda, ground ginger, ground cinnamon, ground cloves, ground nutmeg, and salt until well combined.
4. **Cream Vegan Butter and Sugar:**
    - In a large bowl, cream together the softened vegan butter and brown sugar until smooth and creamy.
5. **Add Molasses and Flax Egg:**
    - Add the molasses, prepared flax egg, and vanilla extract to the creamed butter and sugar. Mix until well combined.
6. **Combine Wet and Dry Ingredients:**
    - Gradually add the dry ingredients to the wet ingredients, mixing until a dough forms. If the dough is too sticky, refrigerate it for 30 minutes to 1 hour.
7. **Roll and Cut Out Cookies:**

- On a lightly floured surface, roll out the dough to about 1/4-inch thickness. Use cookie cutters to cut out desired shapes.
- Place the cut-out cookies onto the prepared baking sheet, spacing them about 1 inch apart.

8. **Bake the Cookies:**
   - Bake in the preheated oven for 8-10 minutes, or until the edges are lightly golden brown.
9. **Cool:**
   - Remove from the oven and let the cookies cool on the baking sheet for 5 minutes. Then, transfer them to a wire rack to cool completely.
10. **Prepare the Icing (Optional):**
    - In a small bowl, whisk together the powdered sugar and non-dairy milk until smooth. Add food coloring if desired.
11. **Decorate the Cookies:**
    - Once the cookies are completely cool, decorate them with the icing using a piping bag or a small spoon. Let the icing set before serving or storing.
12. **Enjoy:**
    - Serve these Vegan Gingerbread Cookies as a festive holiday treat or enjoy them any time of year with a cup of hot cocoa or tea!

These gingerbread cookies are full of warm spices and have a delightful chewy texture. They're perfect for decorating and sharing with family and friends during the holiday season!

# Kiwi Sorbet

**Ingredients:**

- 6 ripe kiwis, peeled and chopped
- 1/2 cup granulated sugar (adjust to taste)
- 1/4 cup water
- 1 tbsp freshly squeezed lemon juice

**Instructions:**

1. **Prepare the Kiwis:**
    - Peel the kiwis and chop them into chunks.
2. **Make the Simple Syrup:**
    - In a small saucepan, combine the granulated sugar and water. Heat over medium heat, stirring occasionally, until the sugar is completely dissolved. Remove from heat and let it cool slightly.
3. **Blend the Ingredients:**
    - In a blender or food processor, combine the chopped kiwis, simple syrup (adjust to your desired sweetness), and freshly squeezed lemon juice.
4. **Blend Until Smooth:**
    - Blend until the mixture is smooth and well combined. Taste and adjust sweetness by adding more simple syrup if needed.
5. **Chill the Mixture:**
    - Transfer the kiwi mixture to a bowl or container and chill in the refrigerator for at least 1 hour, or until completely chilled.
6. **Churn in an Ice Cream Maker (Optional):**
    - If you have an ice cream maker, pour the chilled kiwi mixture into the machine and churn according to the manufacturer's instructions until it reaches a sorbet consistency.
7. **Freeze Without an Ice Cream Maker:**
    - If you don't have an ice cream maker, pour the chilled kiwi mixture into a shallow, freezer-safe dish. Place it in the freezer.
    - Every 30 minutes, remove the dish from the freezer and stir vigorously with a fork to break up any ice crystals. Repeat this process until the sorbet is firm but scoopable, about 2-3 hours.
8. **Serve:**
    - Once the kiwi sorbet is frozen to your desired consistency, scoop it into bowls or cones.
9. **Garnish (Optional):**
    - Garnish with fresh kiwi slices or mint leaves for an extra touch of freshness.
10. **Enjoy:**
    - Serve immediately and enjoy this Vegan Kiwi Sorbet as a refreshing and fruity dessert!

This kiwi sorbet is light, tangy, and perfect for cooling down on a hot day. It's vegan-friendly and a great way to enjoy the natural sweetness of kiwi fruit!

**Vegan Bread Pudding**

**Ingredients:**

- 1 loaf (about 12 ounces) of day-old bread (French bread or any sturdy bread), cut into cubes
- 2 cups non-dairy milk (such as almond milk or soy milk)
- 1/2 cup full-fat coconut milk (from a can)
- 1/2 cup granulated sugar
- 1/4 cup melted coconut oil or vegan butter
- 1 tsp vanilla extract
- 1/2 tsp ground cinnamon
- 1/4 tsp ground nutmeg
- 1/4 tsp salt
- 1/2 cup raisins or chopped dried fruit (optional)
- Vegan whipped cream or ice cream, for serving (optional)

**Instructions:**

1. **Preheat** your oven to 350°F (175°C). Grease a 9x9-inch baking dish with coconut oil or vegan butter.
2. **Prepare the Bread:**
   - Cut the day-old bread into cubes and spread them evenly in the prepared baking dish.
3. **Mix Wet Ingredients:**
   - In a large bowl, whisk together the non-dairy milk, coconut milk, granulated sugar, melted coconut oil or vegan butter, vanilla extract, ground cinnamon, ground nutmeg, and salt until well combined.
4. **Pour Over Bread:**
   - Pour the wet mixture evenly over the bread cubes in the baking dish. Gently press down on the bread cubes with a spoon to help them absorb the liquid.
5. **Add Raisins or Dried Fruit (Optional):**
   - Sprinkle raisins or chopped dried fruit over the top of the bread pudding if using.
6. **Bake:**
   - Bake in the preheated oven for 45-50 minutes, or until the top is golden brown and the pudding is set. It should be slightly firm to the touch.
7. **Cool Slightly:**
   - Remove from the oven and let it cool in the baking dish for about 10 minutes before serving.
8. **Serve:**
   - Serve warm as is or topped with vegan whipped cream or ice cream for an extra indulgence.
9. **Enjoy:**
   - Enjoy this comforting Vegan Bread Pudding as a delicious dessert or sweet breakfast treat!

This vegan bread pudding is moist, flavorful, and has the perfect balance of sweetness and spices. It's a great way to use up leftover bread and is sure to be a hit with vegans and non-vegans alike!

## Chocolate Covered Strawberries

**Ingredients:**

- Fresh strawberries (about 1 pound)
- 1 cup vegan chocolate chips or chopped dark chocolate
- 1 tbsp coconut oil or vegan butter (optional, for smoother chocolate)

**Instructions:**

1. **Prepare the Strawberries:**
   - Wash the strawberries thoroughly and pat them dry with a paper towel. Make sure they are completely dry before dipping them in chocolate.
2. **Melt the Chocolate:**
   - In a microwave-safe bowl or using a double boiler, melt the vegan chocolate chips or chopped dark chocolate until smooth. If using coconut oil or vegan butter, add it to the chocolate while melting to achieve a smoother consistency.
3. **Dip the Strawberries:**
   - Hold each strawberry by the stem and dip it into the melted chocolate, swirling to coat evenly. Allow any excess chocolate to drip off back into the bowl.
4. **Set on Parchment Paper:**
   - Place the chocolate-covered strawberries on a baking sheet lined with parchment paper. This prevents them from sticking and makes cleanup easier.
5. **Optional: Decorate (if desired):**
   - If you want to decorate your chocolate-covered strawberries, you can sprinkle them with shredded coconut, chopped nuts, or drizzle them with melted vegan white chocolate.
6. **Chill and Set:**
   - Place the baking sheet with the strawberries in the refrigerator for about 30 minutes, or until the chocolate coating is set and firm.
7. **Serve and Enjoy:**
   - Once the chocolate has set, transfer the strawberries to a serving plate and enjoy them immediately! They are best enjoyed fresh but can be stored in the refrigerator for up to 24 hours.

These vegan chocolate-covered strawberries are a wonderful treat for special occasions or a romantic dessert. They are easy to make and are sure to impress with their rich chocolatey flavor and juicy strawberry sweetness!

# Maple Pecan Pie Bars

## Ingredients:

### For the Crust:

- 1 1/2 cups all-purpose flour
- 1/2 cup powdered sugar
- 1/4 tsp salt
- 3/4 cup vegan butter or coconut oil, melted

### For the Filling:

- 1 cup chopped pecans
- 1/2 cup maple syrup
- 1/3 cup coconut sugar or brown sugar
- 1/4 cup full-fat coconut milk (from a can)
- 2 tbsp cornstarch or arrowroot powder
- 1 tsp vanilla extract
- Pinch of salt

## Instructions:

1. **Preheat** your oven to 350°F (175°C). Grease or line an 8x8-inch baking dish with parchment paper.
2. **Make the Crust:**
   - In a medium bowl, whisk together the all-purpose flour, powdered sugar, and salt.
   - Add the melted vegan butter or coconut oil and mix until well combined and crumbly.
   - Press the mixture evenly into the bottom of the prepared baking dish.
3. **Bake the Crust:**
   - Bake in the preheated oven for 15-18 minutes, or until the crust is lightly golden brown.
4. **Prepare the Filling:**
   - In a mixing bowl, combine the chopped pecans, maple syrup, coconut sugar or brown sugar, full-fat coconut milk, cornstarch or arrowroot powder, vanilla extract, and a pinch of salt. Mix until well combined.
5. **Assemble and Bake:**
   - Pour the filling mixture over the baked crust, spreading it out evenly.
   - Return the baking dish to the oven and bake for an additional 25-30 minutes, or until the filling is set and the edges are golden brown.
6. **Cool and Serve:**
   - Allow the Maple Pecan Pie Bars to cool completely in the baking dish on a wire rack.
   - Once cooled, slice into bars or squares.

7. **Enjoy:**
    - Serve these Vegan Maple Pecan Pie Bars as a delicious dessert or treat. They are perfect for holidays, gatherings, or anytime you crave a sweet and nutty indulgence!

These bars are rich with the flavors of maple syrup and pecans, and they have a satisfying texture with a crunchy crust and gooey filling. They're sure to be a hit with vegans and non-vegans alike!